EXTREMISTS

STUDIES IN METAPOLITICS

by

JONATHAN BOWDEN

EDITED BY GREG JOHNSON

Counter-Currents Publishing Ltd.
San Francisco
2017

Cover design by Kevin I. Slaughter

Cover image:
Mashup of a photograph of Jonathan Bowden taken by Jef Costello
and elements of two paintings by Carlo Crivelli, *St. Thomas Aquinas*,
1476 (part of the Demidoff Altarpiece), National Gallery, London,
and *Pietà*, 1476, Metropolitan Museum of Art, New York City

Published in the United States by
COUNTER-CURRENTS PUBLISHING LTD.
P.O. Box 22638
San Francisco, CA 94122
USA
http://www.counter-currents.com/

Hardcover ISBN: 978-1-940933-47-4
Paperback ISBN: 978-1-940933-48-1
E-book ISBN: 978-1-940933-49-8

Library of Congress Cataloging-in-Publication Data

Names: Bowden, Jonathan, 1962-2012, author. | Johnson, Greg, 1971- editor.
Title: Extremists : studies in metapolitics / by Jonathan Bowden ; edited by
   Greg Johnson.
Description: San Francisco, CA : Counter-Currents Publishing Ltd., 2016. |
   Includes bibliographical references and index.
Identifiers: LCCN 2016015450 (print) | LCCN 2016026811 (ebook) | ISBN
   9781940933474 (hardcover : alk. paper) | ISBN 9781940933481 (pbk. : alk.
   paper) | ISBN 9781940933498 (e-book)
Subjects: LCSH: Radicalism. | Right-wing extremists. | Political
   science--Philosophy--History.
Classification: LCC HN49.R33 B69 2017 (print) | LCC HN49.R33 (ebook) |
DDC
   303.48/4--dc23
LC record available at https://lccn.loc.gov/2016015450

CONTENTS

EDITOR'S PREFACE

The present book collects transcripts of Jonathan Bowden's lectures on eight Right-wing metapolitical extremists: Thomas Carlyle, Gabriele D'Annunzio, Charles Maurras, Martin Heidegger, Julius Evola, Savitri Devi, Yukio Mishima, and Maurice Cowling, as well as his speech "Vanguardism: Hope for the Future," all of them delivered at the meetings of The London Forum, the London New Right, and similar events.

All of these speeches illustrate three very important truths that Jonathan visited again and again.

First, *metapolitics is important*. "Metapolitics" means that which is above or before politics. Political change can only take place if certain metapolitical conditions are met first. Politics is downstream from culture, as Steve Bannon said. Politics follows pretty straightforwardly from our sense of identity—of who we are and where we are going—our sense of right and wrong, and our sense of what is politically possible. If we can alter what our people think about who we are, where we are going, what is morally right, and what is politically possible—then it will be possible for organized nationalist politics to finally make some headway.

The reason that the political mainstream—both Left and Right—is united in its embrace of multiculturalism and egalitarian leveling is because those ideas are completely hegemonic in the education system, the news media, and the popular culture. The purpose of the New Right is to deconstruct the current anti-white cultural and intellectual hegemony and establish the hegemony of pro-white ideas in its place.

Second, *extremists are important*. Cultural and political innovations take place on the extremes, at the margins, and then are diffused to—or imposed upon—the mainstream. Thus we should treasure extremists. We should cultivate them. We should encourage their creativity. Then we should steal their best memes and spread them far and wide.

Third, *vanguardism is important*. We metapolitical radicals must think of ourselves as the vanguard of our people, as a political *avant garde*. We are the ones who must summon our courage, take the risks, blaze the trails, and lead our people toward their salvation.

Vanguardism must be repeatedly emphasized, because apparently the instinct of every politician is to do the exact opposite. Politicians are inveterate panderers and flatterers of the public mind, which unfortunately has been completely molded by our enemies for generations. Politicians follow the people. Vanguardists seek to lead them. Politicians take public opinion as a given. Vanguardists seek to change it. Politicians always seek to soften their message to appeal to the public. Vanguardists realize this is folly. If one attracts lukewarm followers who are in only partial agreement, then under normal circumstances, you will be fighting with them as much as with your opponents—and when things get tough, they will sheer off and leave you to face your enemies alone anyway.

Thus vanguardists realize that there is no real substitute for the slow, painstaking, and difficult work of converting a significant minority of our people to our way of thinking. We have to uphold a radical and absolute vision and then bring as many of our people around as possible. We should follow the old Roman maxim, "Suaviter in modo, fortiter in re": suave, supple, and infinitely pragmatic and persuasive in style—yet firm and steadfast, indeed adamantine and dogmatic about essential principles.

Jonathan Bowden died in 2012, just short of his fiftieth birthday. But vanguardist that he was, he continues to lead us today, through his recordings, videos, and books like the one before you, always out there on the extremes, not gone—just gone before.

I wish to thank John Morgan, Michael Polignano, V. S., D. K., R. F., Kevin Slaughter, Jez Turner, Lady Michèle Renouf, Max Musson, and Stead Steadman for their help with this project. This book is dedicated to Jonathan's literary executor, Michael Woodbridge, for his responsibility to history.

Greg Johnson
London
May 28, 2017

VANGUARDISM:
HOPE FOR THE FUTURE*

This is a very difficult topic to speak about because it appears to be a depressing and pessimistic era where most of the storm and stress and most of the *Zeitgeist*, or spirit of the age, seems to be against us. There's also a preponderance for people on the Right politically to have metaphysically conservative views, which means they're often pessimistic; they're often loyal to Spengler's idea in the 1920s and 1930s that "optimism is a form of cowardice," and in relation to that sort of idea, the notion that one should be optimistic about the future is difficult to sustain. But given that the past speech was rather sort of statistical and slightly morbid in tone, my job is to not put a reverse spin on it, but at least to attempt to generate some optimistic energy.

Now, there are more of us than ever before, but it's always a question of quality as against quantity in this life, because I think what I'm going to propose is that instead of looking at demographic and quantity-based analyses, quantitative ways of looking at things, let's look at qualitative ways of looking at things. Let's look at quality. Let's look at elitism. Let's look at the fact that all groups need a vanguard.

I remember once a *Times* journalist asked me, a very long time ago in relation to an event called the Le Pen Dinner, which is now twenty years old and more, he said to me, "What's your view of all this stuff about revisionism?" This was in the hotel in Knightsbridge/Kensington where Le Pen and his guests were situated. He said, "What's your view of all that? Is it all true or, contrariwise, is it all false?" And I said, thinking of some famous murder trial of the time, I used the example of the Wests, Frederick and Rosemary now, but of course this particular discussion predated that. "I'd say, well, that trial . . . Is eve-

* This lecture was delivered to the London Forum on December 3, 2011. The transcript was made by V. S.

rything that occurred in that court case all true or all false?" He said, "Well, hold on a minute! Some of it's bound to be true and some of it's bound to be false." And I said, "Well, absolutely. That will go for revisionism as much as anything else."

All that revisionism is, is the ultimate defense of a particular vanguard at a particular time who believe that they were fighting for Western civilization. All elites and vanguard minorities are is the radical consciousness of their own group. And just as people like Louis Farrakhan were mentioned earlier on, who is the leader of a sect called the Black Muslims, and just as they are in some respects totally unrepresentative of a lot of African-American opinion, they nevertheless represent an ultimate redoubt, an ultimate salient, or a bridgehead from which their population can go forth and from which it can gain energy and succor, and that's the way you have to look at these things.

People need ultimate resources. They need absolutists, and they need semi-fundamentalists who will stand up for them, at least in a conceptual way. Even if they can't stand up for themselves, don't want to, or wouldn't even know how to. And the point of radicals, particularly radicals who deal with the politics of identity in any shape or form, is to provide that elite, is to provide that vanguard.

You all know the technology of a bullet, that a bullet is very significant in the impact it can have on a wall or a piece of wood or perforce the human body, but if a bullet is perforated at the top or has mercury injected into the top and is sealed in again, it becomes a far more devastating weapon. It becomes what's known as a dum-dum bullet.

Now, if a vanguard is to have the effect of such retreated bullets, so that conceptually and actuarially the energy and vigor of debate is transformed by the use of such a vanguard and its terminology, it has to be aware of where it's coming from, what its tradition is, where it's going to, and what it represents at a particular time. Just because most of the politics of this era seems to running well and truly against us does not mean that the situation is hopeless, because situations are never hopeless. Groups that have been done down or perceive that they've been done down by history have undergone worse traumas than we are undergoing at the present time.

The danger of the ideology of the victim—which I don't really subscribe to except as a tactic on occasion—is that you begin to think like a victim, and you begin to act like a victim. Many of our people now are almost asking for a whipping, asking for a collective beating, asking to be forgiven for the past, asking to be forgiven for sins and crimes of the past which they never committed, which they're hardly aware of, which could be reconstrued as episodes of heroic cruelty or glorious vanguardism that don't even need to be apologized for in the past or in the present.

And so there's a degree to which I personally think that the doctrine of vanguardism is the way out of the dilemma that we face. All Communist movements believe that the proletariat needed to be saved from itself. They believe that the masses were degraded by feudalism and by capitalism. They believe that only an elite or a vanguard party could raise the masses up to socialism as the inverse of the capitalism they wish to replace. All Communist movements that flourished in Western and other societies throughout most of the late nineteenth and twentieth centuries based themselves on the vanguard principle. These movements were tiny. Smaller than the number of people gathered in this room in central West London tonight by a long way.

I've got a book about literature on my desk at the moment, and in order to tabulate historical reliefs for literary points, they give the listing of events for particular years and in one particular year—I'm not sure, it might be 1912[1]—it talks about the Bolshevik and Menshevik split. It might have been in that year; it might have been in another year. That split happened in London. It happened in a pub in London, and all *Bolsheviki* and *Mensheviki* means is "majority" and "minority." And there was a split between the two of them, and you can imagine them all with their beards and so on haranguing each other and debating about whether there should be an instantaneous rising in

---

[1] It actually took place in 1903.—Ed.

Russia or whether they should wait for the historical process to take its course, because Russia was not yet a capitalist society with a bourgeois class that could be overthrown and so on. The majority of Londoners, even from the ethnic groups that a significant proportion of those Communists were drawn from, would regard all that as idiocy and lunacy, just as the bulk of white people today regard a significant amount of what we say as lunacy.

All people who have a vanguard, an elitist mentality, are regarded as partly mad by their own groups, because the majority of people do not want to know. The majority of people wish to live their own life in their own way, and they only look at these broader questions when life impinges upon them and comes upon them, and the hand of life grasps them by the collar and they really cannot do any other thing but notice what is in front of them.

Many of the reasons our people do not seem to have a sense of solidarity amongst themselves in relation to the degree that some other groups could be said to have is because a significant number of them have never been kicked, have never felt what it is as a group to be disprivileged in a society. Unfortunately, in certain areas of British and Continental life now and North American life, that process for some, and certainly not at the top or middle of the society, is beginning. They're beginning to realize what it's like to be a minority or what it's like to be culturally disprivileged or what it's like to be dispossessed in a way.

Now, that spirit will grow, but it will only feed into consciousness in a number of select minds, because the bulk of people are not drawn to be in a vanguard formulation. People will only listen to a vanguard when they are desperate. They will only listen to a vanguard when they think there is no other hope. They would love for many of the problems of contemporary Britain, many of which revolve around the processes of immigration, to be solved, but they would love to have nothing to do with it themselves, and they would love if somebody came forward magically — without trouble and without fuss — to deal with it on their behalf. They want no unpleasantness, and they want no nastiness, particularly in their own name. But at the same time if somebody does things of any sort that could be ascribed to that, they would run away and hide initially, be privately pleased, condemn the people who did it, support the people who are against them, and yet at the same time have a secret smirk and smile on their face about the whole thing. And they would do all of that simultaneously, and that's what people are like, and that's what our own people are like up to a point, and that's the funk and the state of internal confusion and bemusement that our people are in, because every time they turn on the box in the corner, it says everything is marvelous, and it's all for the best, and that there's no need to worry, and that we're all sleepwalking towards victory.

I read *Nineteen Eighty-Four* again recently. It's been a good quarter of a century since I read that book, and it's a remarkably prescient work in every sense. Of course, it's a social democratic criticism of Stalinist authoritarianism, but in actual fact Orwell's idea that everyone polices their thoughts before they speak, they even police the idea of their thoughts before they speak, is very germane to the present hour.

I was with a relative of mine many years ago, and we were in a wood near Liverpool on our own, and he looked behind him before he made a politically incorrect remark. Because he was worried! He was worried to be alone in a wood with someone else.

And if you remember, in the second section of *Nineteen Eighty-Four*, Julia and Winston have their rather tawdry affair, it has to be said, in a way, against the Party. Sex is rebellion against the puritanism of Newspeak and all that. And they go into the middle of a wood, and they go into a middle of a clearing of saplings in order to get down to it, and the reason that they do that is, one, of course, it's not in an urban area, and therefore there are no telescreens, these televisions that can look both ways with the secret police and the thought police behind them. And on the other hand, there are no microphones, because wherever there isn't a telescreen, you can never vouchsafe that there isn't a microphone, in that particular novel, listening to you.

People are policed now by political correctness, which they adhere to and which they go along with and which they profess to love whilst at the same time hating and despising looking over their shoulder as they refute it and rebut it in the context of their own life. Because that's what the majority is always like. The majority is confused and inane and believes in the last thing that's ever said to them. Of course, in all societies you have a hierarchy of knowledge and understanding. Probably about forty percent of people are quite politically proficient, know what's what, vote to a certain degree, have a cynical regard for the system as it is, at least are *compos mentis* about the sort of culture and society we are living in. But a good sixty percent are not.

There's a famous story about a Labour Member of Parliament who went to a constituent's door. He was Dennis Potter, the playwright that later emerged on the BBC, and he was a Labour candidate in his earlier vintage. And he'd knock on the door, and the woman and husband would come to the door, and the woman would say, "What are you going to do about immigration? As a Labour candidate, as our candidate, as the candidate who will speak the truth to us, unlike the Tories . . ." Not understanding, of course, that Labour is a center-Left party that believes in mass migration as a doctrine of law and morality, and whose Nationality Act of 1948 began the modern-day process of complete societal transformation because, as Attlee said at the time, "If the races of this world were mixed together there will be no more war," and that is an ideology which many of the old Labourites believed in, body and soul, from the anti-colonial movement from which they came. But the bulk of Labour voters thought that Labour stood for something quite different from that. They thought Labour stood for them and for their family and for their extended family, and people who weren't like the people who lived on the posher estate down the way who voted for another party. That's what they thought.

But Potter had to answer this woman and her husband as they stood before him. He said, "Well, what do you mean? Labour is in favor of fairness for all." A politician's answer, of course, even on the doorstep. And she said, "Oh, there's too many, and they're taking over the center of town, and I don't feel safe anymore, and things have changed out of all recognition, and some of what that chap Enoch Powell says—you know, I don't like him, because he's a Tory—but at the same time it's got some truth to it." And all the time Potter was wanting to reply. He was wanting to reply that, "You're a bigot," "I don't want your vote. I don't want it even if you are prepared to give it to me under other circumstances where you said you repudiated what you've just said." And all the time his agent was kicking him, was kicking the back of his heels, as if to say, "Come on. There's plenty of other doors, you know. There's plenty more to do, Dennis. You know, there's plenty to get sort of the red ribbon vote out. Let's leave them to themselves. They'll probably vote Labour, anyway." As indeed they will.

And he kept kicking him and so on, and in the end Potter said, "Labour is in fairness for all, but of course we will listen to your concerns, Madame. We will listen to your concerns." And as he was turning away, the agent said, "And what'll it be then?" to the husband, who had obviously not really gotten a word in beforehand. And the husband said, "Oh yeah, we'll vote Labour as normal, because you listen to what we say." And they're not alone, because there's millions like that. Millions and millions like that. "Politicians will sort it out." "Politicians left to themselves will do something to make sure that things won't get as bad as they could be."

The other thing you often hear about is death. People say, "It's not going to happen while I'm around, therefore I don't need to bother about it." I've had lots of people say to me, "Oh, it's all forty to fifty years off. Who knows what will happen? I can't do anything. You can't do anything. So, what's the point? In any case, I'll be dead by then anyway or gaga or very elderly." And so on. You hear that again and again, because of course what you have in modern Western societies is the extreme powerlessness of the individual. Apart from maybe in consumption and expenditure of cash, the average individual feels totally cut off from the external society. It's what I call deep privatization.

Privatization in the 1980s and the 1990s meant the dispersal of the public utilities and was a sort of Thatcherite and neo-liberal ideology, but privatization has actually gone much deeper than that. It's the view that each is out for himself, and society hardly exists beyond the confines of one's own family, one's own extended family, and people that one happens to know. And people feel not just sort of deracinated, but de-popularized and de-democratized, if there are such terms. And people are, in an extraordinary sense, alone. Alone with the television, alone with the telescreen, which when they flip from channel to channel tells them all the time that everything is perfect, and there are only nasty-minded people who will stir things up as vanguards and various forms of extremism.

Extremism, of course, is something always to be rejected, but I think extremism is necessary. I think it's socially and mathematically necessary, because there has to be a logic to the logic of logic. There has to be something which takes the argument out to the furthest point on the circle. In maths, if you have a curve, you have a line that penetrates it at the furthest extent, and I believe that there has to be a logic that in the realms of sanity and within the realms of what's possible bisects the line at the most radical point, and that's what the people in this room are. That's what vanguard forms of identity amount to. They are the most radical manifestation of the implicit sense of becoming and belonging and identitarian man- and womanhood of the ordinary people in one's own group, and you have to manifest that, and you have to represent it, and only by doing so can you have a certain effect, because you do have an effect by virtue of existing.

There are many other groups on this planet who always ask the question, when anything happens, "Is it good for us?" "Is it good for us, or is it bad for the others?" But most people think actually, "Is it good for us?" Far more people, even of a more vanguard or elitist temperament, are prone to say, "Is it good for us?" rather than "Is it bad for the others?" because, contrary to liberals who always think that positions of identity are based on the idea of doing others down, principles of identity are usually based on boosting or, to use an ugly contemporary phrase, bigging up one's own group. People actually think more positively about themselves before they get into negativity about others, contrary to the view that politics of identity is all about negativity towards others, and as long as you can suppress that through political correctness, everyone can live happily in a multi-cult, multi-identity firmament or melting pot.

I think the point to make about vanguardism is whenever anything happens, people in other groups and people in other vanguards and liberal humanists in our own group, because as the previous speaker said quite truthfully, that it is indigenous liberals who are our real enemy . . . Indigenous liberals are always the enemy. Liberalism within ourselves is always the enemy. It exists even in people who regard themselves as radical, to a certain extent.

We've had liberalism in an uninterrupted way for centuries. Russia's never known a liberal regime, and whether one likes it or not, the politics of contemporary Russia have a lot to do with the fact that they've never known a period of liberalism. You could argue that since the restoration of the monarchy in the 1600s, we've known nothing but various forms of liberalism, most of which linked to various elements of the Protestant religion during that time. But until about the 1950s or '60s, most forms of Protestantism retained residual illiberal and patriotic ideas, as for a period they did in a very sectarian way in Northern Ireland.

So, all views have their liberal side. Even hardliners have their liberal side which they have to guard against, and guard against chipping away at them. Liberalism also feeds on indifference. Indifference to the future and indifference to the generations that are coming in the future.

But vanguardism is something different, because it lives for the virility of what might be in the future. And make no bones about it, what vanguard Caucasians think about their future is watched and is listened to by liberals and by all the other groups. So, the idea that what we do and what we say and what we think has no relevance or no purport is not true. What is true is the competition between groups is part of the stuff of life. And the contemporary society is based upon the formulation that that is not the case, and because it is the case, nature will trump all of the liberal arguments. The problem is that if it doesn't take a political form, nature's trumping of liberalism will be a very painful process to live through, a very painful process for ourselves, for everybody, and for all other persons in other groups. That is why we have to continue with putting forward percussively the politics of identity from our own standpoint.

Let's take something in the news at the moment. There's a large cranking up, and there's a building up of energy for an attack on Iran. At the moment, it appears to be small. It appears to be a cloud smaller than a man's hand. The United Nations has reported that Iran is building a nuclear weapon. The United Nations has reported that their nuclear technology is of dual use, but all nuclear technology is of dual use. When we developed a nuclear weapon the Americans were staunchly opposed to us possessing it, because they wished to live in a unipolar world where only one power had that particular device. Of course, all other major nations were working on these devices. I believe thirty-four other countries are developing some sort of nuclear program at the present time, including Saudi Arabia, because they fear that Iran is doing so, so nearby.

But let's look at it in another way. Is it in our interest that Iran is attacked? Is it in our interest that Iran is attacked? Is it in *our* interest that Iran is attacked? And the answer has to be that it is not in our interest, and it is not in our interest because they're not natural friends of ours, not natural enemies of ours. They exist in a different part of the world, though we exist in a post-imperial situation now. We do not wish to be dragged willy-nilly into yet further wars after Iraq and Afghanistan at America and Israel's behest.

And as soon as one factors into the question vanguardism and group identity, it becomes quite clear that *The Times* and *The Economist* and all of these neo-liberal and neo-conservative journals pushing for an attack upon Iran is not in our interests, and other groups can figure what goes on in the world directly as whether it's in their interests or not.

In a confused way, our people aren't bothered whether

Iran's attacked or not. Our people sit there watching the TV and think, "If the Israelis do it, well . . . I don't know what I think really, you know. Somebody down the pub said it was a good idea. I've got no idea myself. Can they refuel their jets without American help? They'll need American help. If the Americans asked us to help, will that drag us into it?" Most of our people would probably consider, "Is there a danger of a backwash of Islamist radicalism against us because we align against Muslim nations elsewhere on Earth?" which is not a stupid thing to think, actually, and which is probably one of the more credible middle-ranking opinions that people as they sit in front of the television would come out with.

But if our people began to think more in terms of an identitarian prospect, they would nevertheless come to the conclusion that it's not in our interest to attack Iran, and that's just one issue out of an enormous number that could be preconfigured. Is it in our interest to help bail out the euro? Is it in our interest to engage in yet more wars with the United States of America? Is it in our interest to have American bases on our own soil? Is it in our interest to endlessly have a culture of Marxian deconstruction on over all of our media in comparison to what pre-existed the relative social conservatism of the 1950s?

If you slot in all of these ideas, which the masses of people are completely unconcerned about, and yet asked an identity-related question, you come up with the answer that it's not in our interest.

Then you have to switch the questions around and ask, are there certain things which are in our interests rather than against our interests at a particular moment in time? Is it in our interest for a significant proportion of our media to be owned by foreigners? Probably not. Is it in our interest for a considerable part of our media to be owned by pornographers? Probably not. Is it in our interest for much of our banking and for much of our media to be totally international and to have no national specificity at all? Probably not. Is it in our interests that so many of our politicians are part of a jet-set international and humanist class that sees Britain as a puddle to their own self and corporate advancement? No, it's not. As soon as you factor into all of these questions vanguard and elitist propositions on behalf of a group, you come up with an interconnected series of answers about what's in your interest and what's not.

When Tony Blair went to war over Iraq, he said it was in our interests to hug America close, and he was part of an ideology called "Hug Them Close." This is the idea that you never allow, particularly if you're a social democrat in a British context on the right of the Labour Party, any blue water at all between what you and what American foreign policy wants at any particular time, even if privately you don't agree with a lot of it. You still, in a gangster-like way, go along with it.

But is it in our interest to behave in that manner? When we tried to act independently in what may well have been a folly-laden enterprise, which was the Suez operation in 1956, America slapped us down! Smacked us in the face and square in the chops! And we had no particular answer, either. When a run on the pound was engineered by the United States in order to humiliate this country and show it the error of its ways in going for some unilateral action with the French and the Israelis, but not at the behest of American power as it manifested at that particular moment, we were shown what was what. And it's interesting to note that amongst the extraordinary memoralism which is part of contemporary culture, where obscure Olympics are remembered and Manchester United's victories in the '60s are remembered and various other events are churned over by the media, Suez is never dwelt on. Suez is never mentioned. Fifty years on from Suez receives this much attention, and the reason it does receive no attention is because it was a rank humiliation for the then-ruling class in this country, who learned some very salient post-war lessons, and that was that you heel to the United States like an aggressive bulldog and never basically venture to do anything without their recognizance.

And part of the multi-ethnic reconfiguration of these islands is American by proxy, because everything that happens there happens here with a slight time lag, because we have modeled ourselves upon their model of near-open borders and fiscal and capitalist movement of money all over the world, whereby Communist China now controls large sections of the debt mountain that holds up the United States, and where two systems that could be said to be at war with each other ideologically — ultra-capitalist America and post-Communist China — actually have each other in a handshake as well as around the throat, because they now rely on each other to prop each other up in the chaotic world system that now has evolved.

The euro is in desperate trouble, and the Chinese were asked last month to help bail the euro out, and they refused. And quite rightly they refused, because it's not in China's interest to bail out the European economies unless they are reduced to an African level where they can buy country by country!

As you know, China is buying up Africa. They basically say to the black Africans in the sub-Sahara, "Unlike the whites and unlike the Arabs, we've never oppressed you. Let us buy your country!" And they're swarming Africa. Eventually there will be, and there partly are, Chinese cities in Africa. It's not a stupid idea. They will begin running the bureaucracies, they will end up with their own demographic change, and with a smile on their face as they do it, they will take that continent. There's a new scramble for Africa, and it's not Europeans who are doing it. Our time over there, when South Africa went, is gone. The problem is not the dispossession of our colonial elites of the past, but the dispossession of our communities at home in the future and in the present.

But my view is that as long as there is a vanguard to put forward the proposition of an exclusiveness for ourselves, there will always be hope, and that is independent of political parties. Political parties come and go. I believe a new one will be reconfigured in the next eighteen months to two years on the basis of all the splitting which has gone on at the present time. I believe that a new political party is the way forward, but our own people won't vote for it. Not in sufficient numbers, because they're afraid, and because they're in a funk, and because they would like something to happen, but are frightened of the consequences and think that even to mention these things isn't nice. Only a vanguard can mention these sorts of issues, because only a vanguard is unafraid to deal with the thought of not being nice. These ideas afflict and paralyze our people to a degree which is quite extraordinary.

Probably, viewed systematically, more pressure has to be put for there to be more of a radical response. Such pressure is always possible. Economic collapse is always possible. New wars and disturbances are always possible. But one thing we may have to get used to is the idea that, as a group and as an ethnicity, we exist in Europe and North America and Australasia and also all over the world. There are plenty of other groups who see themselves as transnational groups, who see their destiny all over the world. They see their destiny in vanguard terms. They see their destiny as having a core group within their own selves that can come back from anything, genetically and in other ways. Not only do they ask the question when it is asked of them, "Is it good for me or is it bad for me or my group?" They also are prepared to cleave to their own group in times of trouble.

Certain ethnicities have preserved themselves sixty to seventy percent and more genetically since the ancient world, and they have done so by a culture of coherence and identity which crosses national borders and which understands that if a group is to survive, it may need to adopt some radical measures which involve rolling with the blows.

English and British people exist all over the world. We exist all over the world. All over Europe, all over North America, all over Australasia, in quite a few of the countries of Latin America, in most of the ex-colonies. English is the language of the world. It's the *lingua franca* of modernity or post-modernity. We have given the world a great lot, and this is just to refract our own identity through the national consciousness of one particular people who are actually a part of it. So, I think the worst thing that can be uttered at this time is despair, because there are more than enough of us to provide the vanguard which is necessary. The trick is to link the vanguard to the popular will and to find a way to link the vanguard *to* the popular will.

So far, organizationally, in the post-Second World War world, there has been a failure to link the vanguard to the popular will, and that has occurred in all the societies of Western and Central Europe and has occurred even in the post-Communist Eastern European societies where it did appear that such a thing was on the cards immediately after Communism collapsed. It's also true to say that Communism inoculated these populations against the worst and the most noxious forms of liberalism.

The New Right thinker, Tomislav Sunić, who lived under Communism and was imprisoned by it in Croatia with other members of his family, once said that "Communism rots the body, but liberalism rots the soul," and there's a strong degree of truth to that remark, because liberalism attacks on the internal front, on the front of values and identity. It's why the majority of our people refute their vanguardistic yearnings and callings.

Most people, particularly teenage boys, have a sort of yearning for vanguardism when they're early in life, and then they forget it as they get older, and it becomes smeared and smudged over by various forms of liberal orthodoxy. They start either not voting or they vote for one of the prescribed parties: conservative and unionist, liberal democrat, Labour. As long as you remain in that area, you're pretty safe in this country job-wise, career-wise, patrimonially-wise, in terms of reputation, in terms of bourgeois reputation in particular.

If you step outside of those boundaries, and it's quite a wide boundary . . . Liberals would say, "Look, we've given you as wide a space as almost anywhere in the world where you can cavort and make hay and make political pronouncements. Why do you need to go outside that? Why do you need to go out into these extremist and unheralded furrows and sort of support things which are counter-cultural and anti-system?" And the reason that one would choose to do so is because they are not in the interests of the group from which one originates. That's the only reason that one would choose to do so.

The only reason for vanguardism is for the elite to protect the mass and seek to bring it forward in history, because the mass can never act for itself.

In Orwell's novel, *Nineteen Eighty-Four*, which I mentioned at the end, Winston and Julia fail in their rebellion, feeble though it was, against the all-powerful Party, and Orwell wants them to be seen to fail at the end of the novel. But hope lies in the proles, if you remember. Hope lies in the thick-set woman with the laundry basket who's singing a song, "It was only a hopeless fancy." Do you remember that? "It was only a hopeless fancy." As she puts the diapers on the line, she's singing, "It was only a hopeless fancy," which is a prolefeed song given to them by the Ministry of Propaganda in that particular society.

My view is that the future always allies with the elite, not with the mass. The future allies with those that will mold the mass and that will prepare for its energization when a moment comes. That's why my message is one not of despair but of hope for the future, because as long as indigenous, nationally-conscious, ethnically aware, racially aware, inegalitarian, elitist, and other values and views are put forth in a coherent way, in a sane way, and in an educated way — because that's what people expect, views to be put forward in such a way — as long as that happens, there is always hope for the future, because people will align *in extremis* with their own defense mechanism, and they will align with the people who have put forward the defensive barrister's case, which can become offensive as well as defensive in a particular political and social moment.

My view is that as long as there is a continuous effort to put forward the elitist agenda of our own group in the sense that a proportion of people are prepared to place upon their own shoulders the burden of the moral leadership of their own group . . . That's what the Black Muslims do. What the Black Muslims in the United States do is they put themselves forward in the most radical way possible. The bulk of American blacks have no interest in Islam at all and are Christian, and often deeply so, and will only vote for Christian politicians. Yet their most radical vanguard group has adopted Islam, and they have done so because, in their own way of looking at things, they consider it to be a less white, a less Western formulation which is more in keeping with their own sense of their own self, their own strength, their own determinacy.

A similar phenomenon can be found among so-called white extremists where many evince pagan and other views, because they basically want a viewpoint which in their point of view is totally cardinal, and it relates to themselves and to no one else. But that's fine, because all those views do is they sustain the strength of the vanguard. That's why people adopt radical metaphysical views about which many people in this room would argue amongst themselves. But that's not the point. They're the fuel. They're the food. They're the element that keeps people staunch, because it's difficult amongst the withering condescension of a liberal society to maintain elitist identity politics. It's not straightforward, it's not easy, and therefore you need to draw upon certain strengths which are theoretical and which are metaphysical and which are emotional as much as anything else, because one's tie to one's own group has an emotional pull, just as one's tie to one's own regiment, if one's a soldier, has an emotional pull.

That emotional pull is extremely important. The theories are there for the upper part of consciousness and the upper part of the mind. They're also to keep people subtle and to keep people clever and to keep people alert, because if there is such a crisis that our people feel they cannot survive, they will turn to, not us, but to people like us. They always have and they always will.

The crisis in our own hearts and minds is the addiction of our people to liberal answers whilst they remain in zones of economic comfort. That is the problem. Of course, there's all sorts of our people who are not in zones of economic comfort at all, but the problem is that many of them are so degraded by the consequences of life and exist day-to-day, they have no concern with more general and with more theoretical and with sociological changes. They're concerned with this luncheon voucher, this meal tomorrow, this is it to the NHS. They're concerned with what is fundamentally before them at any particular time.

The people you always want in a society are the ones who

have something to lose and the ones who are feeling that they're losing it. This enormous middle that extends from the middle of the middle class to the middle of the working class essentially, the heart of the society, those are the people who have enough of a stake that they're frightened to lose it, and at the moment they cleave to liberalism, because they feel that things are not irretrievably and atrociously so bad that they need to call upon elites or vanguards or forms of identity politics to save them. It's our job to keep pushing the message that they need to turn to their more radical proponents in order to be saved. And all that can really be done at this time is to continue to push that message. Organizations will come and go, but ideas remain, if not eternal, then semi-eternal, and all that we have to do is to keep pushing the message of our own self-belief, of our own form of identity, of our own unique position in history, of our own unique cultural achievements, of the barriers that exist to our own advancement which are in ourselves. Although individuals could be harmed by other groups, the real cause of harm to ourselves is ourselves, our own queasiness, our own moderation, our own love of reasonableness, our own love of seeing the other man's point of view.

All that political correctness is, in some respects, is a growing out of Protestant/liberal apologetics that we want to hear the other man's point of view, that we don't wish to be rude, that we don't wish to be unfair, that we don't wish to be insulting. And these things have been erected into a big engine, into a big, destructive virus that can be used against us to such a degree now that people fear. People fear opening their own mouths.

Everything can be said. Everything can be said. But it can only be said at an abstract and intellectual level, because if you say things at a more guttural or a more primal or a more unindividuated level, you will be arrested immediately under all of the acts which have been passed. If you put things at a high enough level, if you them at the level of a university Right-wing seminar basically, no one can touch you. No one can touch you on Earth, irrespective of all the laws that have been passed.

The only exception would be some of the revisionist legislation in Europe in relation to particular statements, and that applies just to certain European nation-states and not others. But broadly speaking, you cannot be touched. But this means you're talking at an abstract level that alienates you even further from the masses, and which is done deliberately for that effect.

But also remember that everyone knows what you're saying. Everyone knows what is being said, because things are digested at different levels and people absorb things sensually, intellectually, emotionally, psychologically, through the hands, through the heart, through the eye, through the fist. They sense it and hear it at different levels, and everybody understands what is being said even if it's implicit.

Ours is an implicit group. The English are, in part, shy and restrained and even slightly socially awkward. That's why theater is so important in our history, because it gives an alternative space to be others and to be exuberant and to be passionate and to be bombastic and virile, things which are not seemingly part of the national characteristic as is. But everyone understands what is being said. Everyone understands what is happening in this society. Everyone understands the transformation which is being wrought, and everyone understands, or almost everyone understands, the choices that may have to be made in the future.

It's quite clear that at the present time, people are not going to vote for a vanguard party, and there isn't one. But that doesn't mean that a vanguard party shouldn't exist. My view is that a vanguard party should exist and will have to be rebuilt for the moment when such a thing may occur, but the real point is the fact that such a vanguard exists.

Menachem Begin once said that all you needed was two hundred men. For Zionism to be established in Palestine, all you needed was two hundred men who were prepared to act selflessly in the national and ethnic cause and in a religious cause, although his movement was not an explicitly religious one. You don't need many people. When the politics of mass and individual identity come up, you don't need an enormous army of people. What you need is those who have the courage and the will to speak at a particular time and those who keep the mental continuity of that tradition going over time. Because everyone notices what we say, even if it's kept from the masses. Everyone notices what the politics of identity amounts to.

Periodically, there's always a program on the BBC about the far Right of some salacious sort. It's always there. It needs to be there! It's a compulsive need. Why does it need to be there? Because liberals need to scratch. They need to find their opposite half, they need to find their other side, their shadow, their darkness. They need to stare into the pit of darkness. That's what they need! They're in love with this sinister, other side that they project onto.

In Freudian psychoanalysis, there's the idea of projection. Now, let's not get into whether that's a true theory or not, but it's an interesting idea that people who don't like something about themselves project their own nastiness and their own fear and fervor onto others, and that's in some ways what liberals do with people who have, let's call it, nationalistic opinions in Western societies.

They are a product of a sort of secular demonization, aren't they, really? Because the elite that speaks for its own group is treated as the secular equivalent of Satanism, virtually, certainly by many forms of popular media. I mean, that's not an untruthful or particularly biased statement. I think it's just a factual one. Certainly at the level of propaganda, it's a factual one. At the level of academic reportage, it's not, and a more realistic view is taken. But at the level of tabloid media and general media, the demonization is very strong.

And the demonization has worked, which is why people will not vote in enormous numbers for parties of extraordinary reasonableness. All of the populist parties have fallen over themselves to be as moderate and as acclimatizing as possible in this era. They've given away almost seventy percent of the core ultra-views that manifest in these particular areas, and yet still people will not vote for them in a majority way, and that is because the demonization, together with the apathy and the intent of liberalism, have all worked.

But demonization has a point of crescendo. The demonization builds and builds and builds until it gets so out of kilter with reality that people shrug it aside as if it's of no importance, and then it can be a form of virility, and it can become a form of power, and it can be a form of importance.

In Northern Ireland at the moment, the Catholic group is proud to vote for Sinn Féin. Almost everybody. The moderate nationalist party — nationalist in the context of that particular society, don't forget — is dying. The SDLP is an elderly party of trade union activists which is dying.

And there is a degree to which we have to understand that in our politics, all is open and anything can happen, and the future is ours if we want it to be, and that the point of the elitist view that I'm putting forward is that the absence of despair is always necessary for our way of thinking and our way of looking at things. I ask you not to despair. I ask you to look to the future and to the present and to the past. I ask you to remain in faith with vanguardistic and elitist views. I ask you to remain faithful to unpopular views at the present time, because they will become majority views instantaneously at a particular moment if the society should ever break and turn our way. All that can be done is to sustain ideas. One man alone in a room with a computer, a typewriter as it was, can change the world. A few people alone in a room, if they cleave to an idea whose time has come, can still change the world.

There are more of us than ever before. Our people are probably dumbed down to an incredible degree, but more are capable of being better educated than ever before. We're stronger and fitter than ever before.

In the Boer War, when the slums of England were opened, two-thirds of those that came forward were raddled with rickets and disease, and couldn't fight, and wouldn't fight because they physically couldn't fight. Churchill once said, "What's the use of having an empire if you can't flush your own toilet?" One of his rare radical social statements, and there's a degree of truth in all of that.

So, I would ask the people in this room to understand they're part of a tradition, a tradition of non-surrender, a tradition of ultimate resource, a tradition that never says die, a tradition that is the epitome of military life, but in another area theoretically and politically and actuarily. One can never take one's identity from one. One exists for a purpose. Liberals believe life has no purpose, but life has a purpose, and life's purpose is to go forward and to confront that which is before you. And what is before us is cultural dispossession, unless we're prepared to do something about it. What we can do about it will depend upon the circumstances, but what we can do is to remain loyal to our own sense of identity, to our own sense of becoming, to our own sense of what we may be in the future.

Most people are truly afraid. They're afraid to open their own mouths in relation to any of these issues. We must not fear. We must understand that that degree of fear needs to be conquered in ourselves as it will be conquered in others.

Only when the time comes will we be looked to if we remain loyal to our vision of ourselves. We know who we are, we don't know yet where we're going, but we will always exist and we must always maximize the maximum potential of our existence.

There's a book on the side of this room called *March of the Titans*, which in its way hopes to adumbrate all that we have achieved. Our quadrant of mankind has achieved an enormous amount through elite individuals who replicate back onto the majority the success of their own group in architecture, in law, in art, in scholasticism, in morals, in economics, in military affairs, in technology, elsewhere. But also in political leadership, also in military courage, also in vanguardism and elitism.

The present political class has betrayed us, but that doesn't mean that political classes can be done away with. It just means they need to be replaced with people who are better and stronger and more willful and more in tune with the internal vibrations and sense of solemnity of their own group.

I ask you to put your hands together for Britain, for Europe, for Indo-European civilization, for our nation of ourselves, and for an undying and unquenchable fire that can never be put out, because it never knows what it is to be extinguished.

Thank you very much!

THOMAS CARLYLE:
THE SAGE OF CHELSEA*

In many of the speeches that I've given to the New Right since it commenced the better part of three to four years ago, one of my roles—a sort of culturally revisionist role, if you like—is to reinterpret and bring back from the past people who have been forgotten, usually—because I'm bringing them back—I think, undeservedly so. For this talk, I'd like to talk about the great sage of Victorian England, who was a Scotsman called Thomas Carlyle. Thomas Carlyle, one of the greatest writers, thinkers, and orators in print in British literature and British history.

Carlyle has always interested me because of his rootedness in various forms of British tradition, and his melding them linguistically into forms that spoke to his time. The influence that he had over his era is quite extraordinary when one bears in mind that he was trained for the Calvinist ministry but rejected Christian faith in a very complicated and theistic sort of way, but remained a profoundly religious man throughout his entire life and cultural creativity.

Carlyle in his early years didn't quite know what to do with his life. He thought about the Protestant priesthood, and he's rooted in the Protestant tradition in a very radical and transforming manner. He also thought about being a mathematics lecturer and indeed was one for a short time. He then looked at literature and what he could contribute to literature. But he didn't like fictional and poetic forms neat. He wanted to write about philosophical and historical matters, but in a way that was transmuted with a sort of religious energy and an aesthetic zeal. After an early work in mathematics that still exists in an amended textbook form in the United States, he began a long

---

* This lecture was delivered at the fifteenth meeting of the English New Right in London on July 5, 2008. The transcript was made by V. S.

exploration of the cultural channel in the West that was to open up for him his own sensibility, that in turn would ramify with his Scottish and Calvinist roots. This was German literature and German philosophical and Idealist literature from the early part to the middle part of the nineteenth century.

It is not an exaggeration to say that he opened up the British and, in turn, the English mind to Germany and Germanic culture in his era to such a degree that his reputation suffered a great deal during the twentieth century because of his Germanophile nature.

He corresponded directly with Goethe. One of his slogans was, "Close your Byron and open your Goethe." He translated *Wilhelm Meister*, one of Goethe's novels. He translated four volumes of German literature that were published one after the other and that dealt with writers like Richter and with certain of the Idealist schools such as Fichte and Schelling and so on.

In these writers, he saw a way to transliterate the spiritual yearnings that he felt in a way that could be communicated, in a manner that could be understood and appreciated by his era. Born, in some respects, conceptually outside his era, like a seer and a prophet, he came in part to dominate it. He has a strange chronology whereby he begins as an absolute outsider and ends loaded with honors, many of which he chose to reject individually, at the center of his culture, then to be rejected in the early part of the twentieth century because of certain of the authoritarian precepts that he would come to adopt politically in the late to middle period and towards the end of his life.

His first great literary work is the *Philosophy of Clothes* or *Sartor Resartus*, which is designed as an exemplification of Idealist thought, an introduction of what might be otherwise an obscure or arcane area to English and British audiences, listeners, and readers. Don't forget, the number of people who could read fluently then was much smaller than now, and the tradition of one person reading to a group, the oral nature of literature, is extraordinarily important to Carlyle.

Carlyle's prose style has never really been approximated to by anyone else. There is an extraordinary torrent of allusion and inversion, and the use of the dash and the use of epigrammatic insights and a torrent of phrase and of persuasion, nearly always related to a central philosophical idea that underpins the work, or lies to one side of it. Carlyle was a religious thinker in a totally secularizing manner in that he spoke to modernity. He spoke to an age of capital and of machines. He spoke to an age of science. But he used the mechanism of the pulpit and the jargon and language of Knox, which he transmuted in his own mind into a living and sinuous and prosodic form of narrative that he made all his own. "Carlylese" it was called at the time, and no one really has ever written in that way since.

In *Sartor*, he began to satirize nearly all known conditions, partly as a way of clearing the ground from what he thought ought to replace them at a later date. He also served, by virtue of that text, to introduce German Idealist philosophy to an Anglo-Saxon and British audience. He also sought to play games with texts. Introducing one narrative, one autobiographical fragment, then leaving it, describing religious experience such as the one that he's believed to have had on the Leith Walk when he had what for him was a mystical experience whereby he saw the interconnectedness of all things.

Carlyle believed in the reality of God in all areas and at all times, and he believed that all things are interconnected with each other. But in a way, of course, he's reaching way back into the Western and the Greco-Roman tradition. Heraclitus, in his lost book *On Nature* two-and-a-half thousand years ago, believed that energy was the basis of all life and of all being and of all becoming, and that that energy was in some respects flame. And the idea of the interconnectedness of all matter and that which describes it and that which psychologically alludes to it and that which could be said by certain human values to be above it was part of Carlyle's vision. This is why he could write about cultural heroes, he could write about Chartism, a movement of mass democratic and trade union-related reform in the nineteenth century which convulsed the masses of that era and ultimately led, in part, to the democracy we now have in the British Isles.

He could also write about the slave trade. His most controversial text in many ways, which is not reprinted in the Penguin condensed Carlyle, which people are very dubious about in certain respects, laws have been passed which means that even the title of that work I can't mention in a meeting like this, but suffice it to say, John Stuart Mill, his old friend and rival later on, wrote a riposte to it called "The Negro Question," and so you can sort of adumbrate from that what Carlyle was saying and indeed what the title of that work was.

Carlyle believed that life was hierarchical, but that hierarchy had to be based upon the principle of justice. This is why he's uncomfortable reading for the mainstream conservative tradition and for all forms of liberalism and accredited reform. His greatest work after *Sartor* was the multivolume *French Revolution*, the first volume of which was burnt by John Stuart Mill's servant. He was illiterate and thought it was just trash that had been sent to her master, so she said, "Well, this is sorta interesting . . ." and put the whole lot on the fire. You have to understand what that means for a writer in the nineteenth century. There are no word processors. There are no "I'll stick it in this window and give this chap a disc to see what he thinks of it." The whole first volume was burnt. This was a blow to Carlyle, it really was. When Mill came to see him he was white, white as a sheet. And he should have been, to be frank. He offered Carlyle a hundred pounds, which was a lot of money in the nineteenth century, to rewrite the first volume, and for a while Carlyle was stuck, but he soon got into the nature of the work.

The French Revolution is one of the most extraordinary books of the nineteenth century, because for a moment, we have to reposition ourselves in that time. For people towards the middle of the nineteenth century, the French Revolution was an unbelievable experience, which had not, never mind revisionism, been assimilated into the knowledge of the middle of the nineteenth century. The terms Left and Right, most of the language and discourse that we use in contemporary politics all over the West, originates from these extraordinarily tumultuous events which began with quite mild origins towards the later phase of French monarchicalism in the eighteenth century. The nineteenth century remained deeply worried by the chaos and revolutionary ardor and violence that was released at the end of the previous century.

Carlyle, unlike almost all other historians, who tend to adopt a prosaic, measured, stoical, Johnsonian period in language and in sensibility . . . History should not be written in white passion. History should not be written in a committed way, committed not to one side or the other, but committed to the virility and vitality of the thing itself. History, in a sense, should be rather like Gibbon's *The Decline and Fall of the Roman Empire*. It should be judicious. It should be slightly acidic. It should be neutral. Carlyle is never neutral! Carlyle speaks with radical Protestant and even re-Aryanized Old Testament fury! Carlyle is always right. And he was an ideologue and in some ways a literary demagogue, and the Victorians were dying for it. Because internally, under all their progress and all their science and all their industrialism and their vouchsafed Christianity, they were uncertain. They wrote enormous encyclopedias to docket in a taxonomic way everything, so that everything could be secured and put in its place. But deep down, as Nietzsche analyzed at the end of the nineteenth century, there was a great subconsciousness of doubt.

Carlyle never had any doubt, but he was not a prater who reached any opinion whatsoever like a barrack room bore. He believed, actually, in the dialectic of silence for long periods before you spoke.

In *The French Revolution*, he believes that the *ancien régime* was rotten and that divine judgment was given on France in relation to the revolutionary period. Not a conservative or a sort of Right-wing reactionary or monarchical viewpoint. There's a review in France called *Rivarol*, which dates from before the Revolution and which later became submerged in the literature of Jean-Marie Le Pen's movement, and this is a sort of Whiteist or counter-revolutionary documentation that straddles two hundred years. These were people who were to the Right of the Right before the concept of Right was thought of.

For those not entirely in the know, in the French Revolution, when you formed an Assembly, the center would be the chairman and those who were stood in the middle or sat in the middle. Those to the right of them were those who wanted to conserve the status quo that revolutionary change had reached., Not the status quo, and not the prior monarchical arrangement, but the status quo that the revolutionary spasms had reached. Those who were to the left of the chair, the destructive side, as Carlyle calls them, wanted reform. All of our terminology of Left and Right, even though they relate to certain metaphysical and occultistic ideas that predate modernity, nevertheless originates here, and in the belief that the French Revolution is cardinal to Western history. Carlyle achieved a great work, a work of art which is a work of historical science, a work of scholarship, yet a work of passion, the bringing together of things which are thought really never to go together properly.

If you read Carlyle now, you sense an explosion of sensibility, particularly when he's dealing with The Terror, dealing with the march of the women to Versailles, when lots of revolutionary men dressed as women go to Versailles to bring back the King, the extraordinary bread riots in the early years of the Revolution, and the storming of the Bastille. Carlyle always uses the present tense, always hammers away! You're there! You're right in the middle of it! History's real! Men are being slung to one side; the tumbrel is rolling; heads are off and on pikes. It's happening before you.

If you've ever seen the silent film from the 1920s, which has significantly fascistic undertones, called *Napoléon* by Abel Gance, you almost get in those seething crowd scenes and the split use of the screen, which splits into three by the tricolor at the end, you sense the dynamism and movement of Carlyle's prose. The belief that literature isn't a dry, academic discourse that's shut off with nerdy people to one side of life. It is living and cauterized and molten and ferocious! Because, in a way, his view of the divine is a sort of Protestantism that reaches to a pagan conclusion in spite of itself.

The radical nature of Protestantism and its intellectual impact on Anglophone societies, such as Britain and the United States, the reason why culturally we are differentiated from much of Continental Europe is because of this intellectual inheritance. One of the interesting things about Carlyle now is that we often think of elements of the post-Protestant tradition, which has led to the liberalism that's all around us, as a burden. Many people in Britain who have radical Right views are often Roman Catholics or lapsed ones or extremely authoritarian ones. Or they're pagans. Or they have no faith at all. Interestingly, that Protestant middle, particularly that Anglican soft middle, if you like, is often radically underrepresented. And yet in a way, although it's Calvinistic in origin, Carlyle's diction and attitude and mentality enables us to look in a positive way at elements of the radical individualism and granite-like metaphysical objectivism and authority of purpose that a *profound* individual mind can have.

Protestantism, in a sense, has two distinct roads to travel from his day to ours. One is the liberal modernity that exists all around us. If you want to see it, you just go out into Holborn now. The other is a reconnection with the Greeks and the world that existed even before Christianity. You explode into Carlyle and Kierkegaard. You explode out into Nietzsche. You explode out towards the end of the nineteenth century, outside of Christianity itself.

But these essentially were constructive men. Carlyle loathed the destructive in the human mind and in society. That's why he's deeply an anti-Leftist thinker if he is anything. The Revolution revealed an enormous panoply of destructive energy. But he believed that it's the purpose of leadership to galvanize, to straddle, and to direct those energies when they occur.

One of the criticisms that's been levelled against Carlyle's books as they go on after *The French Revolution* to reposition, reevaluate historical figures, to write about the movements and social ideologies of his time, to engage in a form of revisionism in relation to Muhammad, in relation to Oliver Cromwell, in relation to all sorts of figures who in some ways were minor cultural hate figures in his era that he got people to look at again in another way in the teeth of much cultural opposition. Gradually, he split from many of his liberal friends, such as John Stuart Mill, with endless denunciations of utilitaria, as he called it.

One of Carlyle's great strengths is his belief that language is a *new* thing. You don't necessarily go against the order of grammar. But a genius *reinvents* in the crucible of creation. He developed more words, more neologisms than almost anyone in his time.

He also, in his book about slavery, pointed out that half of the white children who lived in Britain at that time died before they were five. And yet moralists and idealists, many of them factory owners, were concerned about the West Indies. In some ways, that tactic of textual refusal and aggression is part of an old Tory satirical tradition.

The text that most reminds me of his book about slavery — which I think was published in Edinburgh's *Fraser's Magazine* in 1849, I'm remembering from memory here — is Swift's *Modest Proposal* that the Irish, in relation to the prospect of famine, should eat their own young cannibalistically. That is often interpreted in a literal-minded way when, of course, these thinkers are often extremely metaphorical and wish to throw ideas upon a canvas in order to bring things out more starkly and with greater aesthetic virility.

It was quite funny actually, because in the 1970s RTÉ, which is the broadcaster in the south of Ireland, broadcast Swift's *A Modest Proposal*, and it led to a fistfight among literati in the studio as they rolled around because they interpreted it as a literal insult against the Irish people, when in actual fact it's an attack on British policy in Ireland. That's the danger that you get into when you use politics as metaphor and as extreme literary statement.

But Carlyle loved being incendiary. He loved dialectic, divisiveness in debate. He, in a sense, luxuriated in conflict. And in the latter stages of *The French Revolution*, you sense a tension, particularly when he deals with the late period of the Terror, which he sees always as a judgment upon France and upon the French and *in extenso* upon the West.

Many of his phrases that historians use now were coined then. The notion that Robespierre is sea-green in his incorruptibility. When Robespierre was dragged to the guillotine with a smashed mouth and with his brother in tow and with the other terrorists with him, the terroristic adolescent Saint-Just, a crippled Couthon who wanted to guillotine everyone else, and when they were all dragged by the Thermidorian Reaction to the scaffold, the tumbrels were beating, Robespierre went under the guillotine, the mobs that had cheered the ones that he'd done down, including his own revolutionary colleagues Camille Desmoulins, slightly to the Right of Robespierre's factions, the Advertists of the Paris Commune and town hall slightly to the Left. Carlyle is there as real novelistic presence in history.

Contemporary academicism, which in a strange way, because of various postmodern ideas which have been current in the West for the last thirty years, now elevates Carlyle to a new status, have always feared his partiality, the fact that there is no neutrality in his view of creation, because he believes that all creation is divine, that it is all interconnected and that it all has a meaning and purpose. The problem, as Nietzsche would have pointed out later, is perspectivalism. It may all have a meaning and purpose, but almost each coherent and literate historian will attribute a different one to it.

Carlyle leaves many of those problems unresolved. But in his idea of open-mindedness towards the text and towards history and towards historical documentation, there is something extraordinarily liberating. History is regarded as a subject, by many people, as a bore, something to get through, something which isn't really alive, something that doesn't relate to them. The interesting thing about him is his belief in its living quality. These people are speaking ethical lessons to us from the past, but they're as alive as we are now.

Now, as he became the sage of Victorian England, and as he excoriated Victorian capitalism and laissez-faire individualism more and more, many of his more liberal-minded friends from the early days began to move away from him. It's important also to realize that by the middle of his life, he was a cultural lion. He knew virtually everybody who was of any significance in the culture of his day. Dickens used to carry around a multi-volume set of *The French Revolution* and once told a friend, "When I want to think something, I just fish it out and have a look at one of the volumes." It had a totemic effect on many people in the era in which he was alive. And bearing in mind, this is a man who would later be cynically put down by the Bloomsbury Group at the beginning of the twentieth century as an uneducated Scotch peasant lecturing to the rest of us on the basis of his extreme Protestant morality.

Carlyle became a partly demonic figure in the twentieth century because he's regarded as proto-fascistic. The last book Hitler ever read was his six-volume history of Frederick the Great, and Frederick the Great's ability amidst chaos on the battlefield to construct endless forms of order. The interesting thing about Carlyle is he thinks that micrologically and at the lowest possible level, and in a grain of sand, the universe entire is revealed. So, an individual decision made by a general or monarch on the battlefield has relevance to the way in which you make decisions about the ordering of energy in society way outside of the area of the battlefield or even the war that they are actually fighting, the result of which to his way of thinking is often less important than the cardinal, ordinating or prior principle which an authoritarian leader of genius brings to the chaos of creating new forms.

In a way, he has a sort of titanic and alluvian view. He's less concerned about the ideological niceties of Oliver Cromwell, of Muhammad, of Shakespeare as a cultural leader than their ability to corral and to restore and to give energy to certain circumstances, to bring energy into fruition in texts and human behavior. One of the reasons why the postmodernists and post-structuralists, who were a school in late twentieth century academicism, particularly in the arts, like him is because of his open-mindedness to the interconnection between texts and life and the ability to see texts as living and volcanic documents.

During his high middle period, he produced a whole series of texts such as *Past and Present* and *Heroes and Hero Worship* and *Latter-Day Pamphlets,* in which he looked at almost every element of contemporary Victorian life—he looked at slavery; he looked at democracy; he looked at imperialism; he looked at the emancipation of women; he looked at extremities of poverty and wealth; he looked at industrialization and laissez-faire economics, which was then becoming *de rigueur.* He believed that the modern world would become atomized, would be-

come spiritless, would become falsely individualist, would become completely material, and would lose its connection with
what he perceived of as the divine.

His attitude towards religion is complicated, deeply personal, rooted, and idiosyncratic. He does believe in a spiritual dimension beyond life, which he believes he's actually experienced in a personal revelation. He could have only experienced
it as a personal revelation, because in a sense such a viewpoint
is so personal that it's truth-positive, can't really be communicated. The effects of that experience on Carlyle, the belief that
everything is interconnected, means that the smallest and the
highest moment are of equal significance to the possibility of
the whole, even in their inequality. He believes that unfairness
and inequality are rooted as part of nature and natural becoming. Does he believe that God is nature? Not entirely. He's not
totally pagan in that way. His conception, as far as I can see it,
is a metaphysical objectivism where there are certain criteria
(beauty, truth, justice) that lie outside man and prior to man.
And, like most of the religious thinkers of the past, these are
objective in that they are not perspectival and they can't be reduced to contemporary human standards. But, very like Nietzsche in a way, the way in which we perceive these absolutes,
the foreknowledge of which we can't have any idea of in our
own personhood, in our own individuality, is to strum towards
truth and becoming in the moment in which we find ourselves.

When the peasant demands bread at the height of the riots
when the physiocratic economic system was collapsing just
prior to the Revolution of 1789, he is demanding, in Carlyle's
view, justice in his society. The point of aristocracy is to rule in
accordance with laws and the development of the creative evolution of human society. If a ruling group fails in its obligation
to rule, all the privileges and the flummery that go with it,
which means very little to a Spartan conscience like him, goes
by the way and they're cast aside by history, and a new group
is brought in. Carlyle is not a conservative, but in some respects
is a revolutionary conservative of a sort. So, the idea that a
leadership can fail and needs to be dispensed with, the opposition in a sense to what you might call an English Tory view

that no matter how bad it is, a leadership should always be kept going because it is bound to be slightly better than what might replace it: Tolstoy's view that revolutions are always the worst because they come to power new and hungry, and you don't quite know what they're going to do.

Carlyle believes in the prospect of absolute change, but it is change rooted in tradition, which if it devours its own children like the Greek titans will prove to be worthless in the way that the Montagnards were useless and worthless, in his opinion, at the end of the French Revolution.

The Montagnards were The Mountain in the Convention, the most revolutionary of the French revolutionary assemblies. The first was the *ancien* monarchical regime, the *ancien régime*, with its estates. The Third Estate was the first assembly. Then you had the Constitutional Assembly morphing into the Legislative Assembly. Then you had the French Assembly, to this day it's called the National Assembly, of course, and is rooted in the ideas of this period. Then you have the Convention, the one that all students of this period, if they ever read this period at school, understand. The Convention consists of the moderate revolutionists to one side of the chair, the Right, the center sweeping into the Left and the extreme Left. They were called The Mountain because they had the highest seats. And in the highest seats there was Maximilien Robespierre, there was Danton, there was Desmoulins, there was Couthon, and there was Saint-Just. There were the others. The *terroristes*.

Robespierre began with a pamphlet saying he abhorred the death penalty and ended up synonymous with its use. At the high point of The Terror, one thousand two hundred, one thousand four hundred were being physically guillotined in the center of Paris, including many of his old revolutionary colleagues. And he would stand there with a perfumed handkerchief and mop his brow and mop his mouth and say, "It's for progress! It's for liberation! It's for France!" Because don't forget, many of the forms of extreme Leftism that existed at that time were infused with nationalism and with national power. Until the middle of the nineteenth century, certain liberal ideas and nationalism of course went together against traditional, conservative, monarchical forms of order. Within decades, nationalism and liberalism would become dire political enemies.

Carlyle is writing at a time not of confusion, but of voltaic energy and becoming. His revisionism about Cromwell is truly extraordinary, because Cromwell was unbelievably hated at the time that he began on *Oliver Cromwell's Letters and Speeches* and his attempt to exemplify them.

It's interesting the way he often deals with texts. In *Sartor Resartus*, there's the sort of text which he stands to one side of, plunges into the middle of. His transubstantiatory religious experience at the Leith Walk is actually deeply embedded in the middle of that text, but it's presented in some ways as though it's happened to somebody else. In his book on slavery, it's a document that's left for somebody else to find. These are extraordinarily modernist and postmodernist experiments in using your own voice, throwing your own voice as a form of cultural ventriloquism, speaking through other people. In *The French Revolution*, he allows everyone to act.

Do you remember those old films of the Soviet revolution by Eisenstein and these sort of people? They're almost like puppet films. They're amazing and silent. You have the masses speak, and they wave their fists in the air, and then they run in one direction. In *Battleship Potemkin*, the sailors run to one side and then run in another area. It's almost as if there is an attempt to make Marxist theory and the idea of historical progress real at the point at which masses move and act. There's this extraordinary moment, just as cinematography, where the nurse holds up the dead child and she herself is shot by the White troops in *Battleship Potemkin* on the steps as the soldiers come down with their bayonets. And I always sense there is something pre-cinematic about Carlyle's writing about history.

Now, in the repositioning of Cromwell, he's not concerned about certain ideological matters that might interest people here about Cromwell. He's interested in the idea of a man, particularly that comes out of the extreme Protestant dispensation, an Englishman, of course, an English revolutionary, who changes the reality of his society and his time through an act of will and does so in relation to foregrounded moral ideas. Political action which is not based upon personal conviction, to Carlyle, is always worthless and better not to try.

Now, as his career goes on, he becomes more of a sage, more looked to, more hostile to the extreme forms of capitalism that are developing all around him in England. One of the most extraordinary things about him, although Dickens does it as well to a degree, is he's so aware of the raw energy of England then like China now. Pollution everywhere, exploitation everywhere, enormous amounts of wealth everywhere, extreme poverty everywhere. The radicalism of that society and its sort of striving and creation of gold out of the ground and new classes of men, tough-faced men from the north of England and elsewhere, who were titans. Theodore Dreiser wrote a book in the early part of the twentieth century in America called *The Titan* about these entrepreneurs and factory owners who almost come from nothing, and within one generation they're sitting in Parliament, peers, calling the shots for the entire society and its empire.

Carlyle was an imperialist, but he believed it should be based upon certain moralities of form. He was a nationalist in certain respects, and yet at the same time his feeling for nationality was very complex and aesthetic, very much like Kipling's in "Recessional" in many ways. A profound reactionary and yet rebellious spirit whereby you looked at things, sought to meld them and move them in accordance with the energy of the hour, and always sought to find divine purpose in the actions of men. When he found that there wasn't such, he moved away, or he didn't give it cultural endorsement.

A great talker, a great raconteur. A great celebrity in a period where celebrity meant something slightly different than what it means today. There's a famous incident he once shared. A woman in a salon said to Carlyle, "I do believe, Mr. Carlyle," she said, "in the idea of the interconnectedness of the universe." And Carlyle rumbled in reply, "You better," in a Scotch accent, because he was quite a character. He was the most extraordinary religious and literary incendiary that this society produced in the nineteenth century.

Now, towards the end of his life, he wanted to find one ruler in relation to the chaos of Victorian modernity who he could posit as a counter-balance and weight. Frederick the Great of Prussia was, for him, in his ideological way of looking at the literary texts of his own of that monarch's life, a way of exploring the idea of benevolent dictatorship. Carlyle is opposed to democracy. Carlyle doesn't believe in rule by majority. Carlyle doesn't believe in coherent, stratified, old-style rule by aristocracy, certainly not an aristocracy that does not reform and certainly no aristocracy that has no concern paternally for the plight of the people, particularly at the bottom. His sort of socialism, socialistic, and solidarist beliefs are inegalitarian and always elitist, because morality and will and vigor and power comes from above to below in all areas of life. But those at the top have to be worthy of ruling those at the bottom. Otherwise, in his opinion, they will be judged by history.

As he got older, he became, in contemporary terms and in terms that he used himself, more and more Right-wing. And he prefigures some of the authoritarian social movements of the twentieth century, for whom in many ways he was an illuminating character. It's interesting to note that many of the great figures (Arnold, Ruskin, Morris), many of them alleged champions of the Left (many a faceless tower block called Morris Block or something was put up by old Labour in the 1960s and so on), yet in many ways these Romantics, these socialists, these conceptual pre-Raphaelite types, these neo-Medievalists, were actually looking back to past orders of social organicism. They weren't looking forward to the modern Left. They were actually, in some ways, quasi-Right-wing individuals who have been falsely positioned as neo-Leftists in the early part of the twentieth century.

Carlyle is part of the authoritarian, Right-wing tradition. He's also a figure that uniquely can be used in British terms, in British circumstances. Many people who are just concentric to these islands wonder where our "Nietzsche" is, where our figure of indomitable literary power and glory might be, where our combination, if you like, of Jack London and Nietzsche in certain respects, where our figure is.

As a modest proposal of mine, unlike Swift's, would put

forward the idea of Thomas Carlyle as a man who in the translations of German Idealism, in his book upon the philosophy of
clothes which rips them away and shreds utilitaria and demands a spiritual dimension to the complications of early nineteenth-century life, to his analysis of the French Revolution as
the climacteric of that period, of the period in which his sensibility was formed, in relation to his desire to even preserve the
existence of slavery whereby he looked back to the ancient
world and analyzed the enormous numbers of forms (don't
forget, serfdom in Russia wasn't abolished until the 1860s) that
inequality and service takes in all forms of societies (ancient,
modern, and Medieval), in his attempt to explicate the Medieval world, where he sees in a Medieval abbey a sort of integrat-
edness of life, a solemnity and a stoicism of purpose that
moderns lack.

The modern society for many is alienated, is broken down,
is inorganic, is increasingly meaningless. The great thing about
a lot of these nineteenth-century sages is that they're talking to
us. They are talking to what, internally, the modern West has
become even though they are one hundred, one hundred fifty
years "out of date." The interesting thing is the most advanced
European intellectuals realized many of the crises that were
going to come for our civilization long before it began to dawn
on mass consciousness: that our old religion would collapse,
that, as Nietzsche said at the end of the nineteenth century, that
will be a liberation, certainly for certain elite spirits, but it will
also be a great burden for the majority, because it has left them
bereft. It's left them with nothing. It's left them in the culture of
the ruins and the ruins of culture.

The extreme Right in the twentieth century was one of the
formulations whereby we attempted to reconstitute certain of
the wholeness that existed in the modernity which has come
down to us. An extreme alliance of bedfellows, who were completely at variance with each other as their subsequent warfare
showed, namely the ultra-capitalist, most Western powers of
all and Communism, combined to destroy it. And we are in
some ways culturally amidst hyper-modernity, living in the
ruins.

But Carlyle's work, from his analysis of the stoicism and mental and moral and linguistic integration of the Medieval abbot in comparison to a modern factory owner, to his hostility to modern democracy, where the masses are bought and sold shoddy packages and lied to perpetually by politicians who change their opinion in an instant, in parliaments that have little or no moral integrity and are based upon no philosophical precepts at all, in relation to an aesthetics and an architecture which even in his era he perceived as inferior to the past, he speaks to us now through his revolutionary energy, through his use of Protestant diction, for his respect for the individual.

The Western culture begins and ends with a supreme individual mind. It's partial. It's nominalist. It's perspectival. It looks at life from the perspective, hopefully heroic, of a coherent individuality. It often doesn't say it has the whole truth, but it is participatory to the explication and evolutionary revelation of the prospect of the truth. And these men are the great geniuses of our civilization. They don't have every answer, but they open up a plenitude of partially answered questions the nature of which you need to completely resolve before you can step on to something more.

All of our great thinkers are shooting arrows into the future. And Carlyle is one of them. Thirty books, not including the reminiscences of his wife, Jane Carlyle, not including paraphernalia and the biography he never wanted to have written, not including the notes, apocrypha, and letters. The enormous Herculean energy to produce that in the teeth of much cultural opposition of the time. Don't forget, he was denouncing what liberal Victorian values were: industrialization, ugliness, contempt for the environment, contempt for what he perceived to be the spiritual dimension of man.

He's not concerned with suffering, because suffering can ennoble. But it's the meaning that's attributed to it and the feeling that industrialization, the suffering of the masses, have been rendered somehow meaningless. It's the sort of aesthetic squalor, with its attendant moral bankruptcy, which appalled him. He is a moralist, but the interesting thing about the great thinkers in our tradition is he's not a moralizer. He's not wagging his finger. He's excoriating! He's a sort of man on the mountain who is telling you what he thinks.

At the end of *Zarathustra*, Nietzsche says this Persian sage of old comes down from the mountain and walks in the valleys prior to going up into the mountains again. Why does he choose Zoroaster, or Zarathustra? Because he's a dualist and because Nietzsche wants to overcome dualism. So, he uses one of its oldest Aryan spokesmen to overcome that particular rigidity in thought. Zarathustra has two pets: a snake and an eagle. And the eagle is courage, and the snake, sometimes a synonym for sexuality in most cultures, stands for knowledge.

Knowledge and courage! What does a man need in this life but knowledge and courage? And then he goes out into the morning to experience a great noontide. Not the end of the day, not the sorrow and the tiredness of the dark, not yet the beginning, but the noontide when the Sun is up and life is golden and there is a future. And many of our great thinkers contribute, step by step, to the nature of that future.

All of Carlyle's texts now exist on the Internet and other forms. There are American paperback editions of nearly all of them bound together, from the translation of the Germanic Idealists through to an analysis of John Knox and the Norwegian kings, through to his analysis of the people that he knew in his own life, to his own personal relationships, and to the nature of the French Revolution, an extraordinary text.

When I did A-level history, you were taught Soboul, who is a Trotskyist, and you were taught Lefebvre, who is a Marxist, and you were taught Jaurès, who is a nineteenth-century socialist, occasionally some conservative, Burke or whatever he was called, would be allowed in to sort of wave a sort of white flag for the *ancien régime* before being silenced. But nobody ever even mentioned Carlyle and his revolutionary and impressionistic work, *The French Revolution*. It exists in paperback in Cambridge University Press, in the Oxford University Press Classics. *Sartor* does as well. All of the books are available. There's an excellent hardback bibliography by that uniquely American school of the sort of Oxford University Press, where a German-American scholar with extraordinary refinement and passion and attention to detail details every book that was ever published under Carlyle's name and/or in print in the nineteenth century. This work is all available, and it's heroic and vitalist literature.

He's too opinionated for anyone to agree with, and he's the sort of person that you will occasionally read and you will want to throw the book across the room. But that doesn't matter, because he *wants* that response. He would prefer radical negation than indifference. Because in his way of looking at things, pantheistically up to a point, indifference is the worst form of hatred.

So, I give as an Englishman the great Scottish genius, Thomas Carlyle. Read him and know more.

Thank you very much!

GABRIELE D'ANNUNZIO*

Gabriele D'Annunzio had basically two careers, one of which was as a writer and literati and the other was as a politician and a national figure. If you look him up on *Wikipedia*, there's a strange incident which occurred in 1922 when D'Annunzio was pushed out of a window several floors up in a particular dwelling and was badly injured and semi-crippled for a while. And of course, this was during a crucial period in Italian politics because Mussolini emerged as leader of the country and was made Prime Minister after the March on Rome under a still-monarchical system and absorbed and swallowed up all other Italian parties to form the Fascist state in Italy that lasted right until the end of the Second World War.

Now, D'Annunzio as a figure was involved in the Romantic and Decadent movement in Italian literature. He wrote a large number of plays, quite a large number of operas, a large number of novels, and some short story collections. He was too controversial ever to be awarded something like the Nobel Prize, but at the beginning of Italy's twentieth-century period, he was one of the most popular people in Italy. Almost everyone had an opinion about him, and almost everyone had heard of him.

His work combines various pagan, vitalist, and Nietzschean forces, and he was heavily influenced by Friedrich Nietzsche and his philosophy. Some of his works were banned on grounds of public morals, both in translation abroad and in Italy *per se*. *The Flame of Life* was one of his more ecstatic and Byronic celebrations of life. *The Triumph of Death* was another of his works, and *The Maidens of the Rocks* was another one, and a poem called "Halcyon," which was part of an interconnected series of poems five in number. He was going to write a larger collection than this, but those were the ones that got done. Also, he celebrates the Renaissance period and the period of Ital-

---

* This lecture was delivered to The London Forum on January 21, 2012. The transcript was made by V. S.

ian greatness when Italian civilization became synonymous with Western civilization, and indeed looked to put its stamp upon world civility.

So, D'Annunzio brought together a wide number of strands which supervened in Italian politics and culture since the unification of Italy under Garibaldi in the nineteenth century. Like Germany, Italy was unified as a modern European nation-state quite late in the day, and a triumphant sense of national vanguardism, identity, and pressure and force was always part of D'Annunzio's ideology.

Superficially, it seems strange that you have artists of extreme individuality like Maurice Barrès in France in the 1890s, who wrote a book called *The Cult of the Self* (*Le Culte du Moi*) along Nietzschean and Stirnerite lines and professed a very extreme individuality, who were also ardent nationalists. And this is because this cult of the heroic individual and this cult of the masculinist and this cult of the superman and the cult of the pagan individual that D. H. Lawrence's novels in English literature could be said to be part and parcel of, at least at one degree, that went hand in glove with the belief in national renaissance and national glory. The great individual was seen as a prototype of the great man of the nation and was seen as a national leader in embryo, whether or not the work took on any political coloration at all. So, what appears to be a collective doctrine and what appears to be an individualistic doctrine marry up and come together and cohere in various creative ways, and this was part of the cultural tension of the late nineteenth century.

D'Annunzio is a nineteenth-century figure who explodes into the twentieth century by virtue of mechanized politics. Debts and the pursuit of various people to whom he owed money because of his extraordinarily lavish and aristocratic lifestyle led D'Annunzio to live in France at the time of the outbreak of the Great War, but he soon hurried back to Italy in order to demand Italy's entry into the Great War on the Allied or Western or Tripartite side. Of course, in the Great War, Italy fought with the Western allies, with France, with Russia, and with Britain against Germany, the Austro-Hungarian Empire, and the Ottoman or Turkish Empire in the convulsive conflict which people who lived through it thought would be the war to end all wars.

D'Annunzio had an extraordinary war. He joined up when he was around fifty years of age and gravitated towards the more aristocratic arm of the three that were then available. It's noticeable that the war in the air attracted a debonair, an individualistic, and an aristocratic penchant. Figures as diverse as Goering in the German air force and Mosley in the British air force and D'Annunzio in the Italian air force all fought a war that, in its way, had little to do with the extraordinarily mechanized armies that were fighting on the ground.

You had this strange differentiation between massive armies and fortifications of steel with tunnels turning the surface of the Earth like the surface of the Moon down on the ground until tanks were developed that could cut through the sterile nature of the attrition of the front—a very static form of warfare from 1915 until the war's end in 1918—and yet above it you had this freedom of combat, this freedom in the air with biplanes which were stretched together from canvas and wood and wire and were extraordinarily flimsy by modern standards, without parachutes for the most part, and where the men often used to often fire guns and pistols at each other before machine guns were actually fixed to the wings so they can actually fire on each other in flight.

There was a cult of chivalry on all sides in the air which really didn't superintend with the massive forces that were arrayed against each other on the ground, and this enabled a spiritual dimension to the war in the air that was commented upon by many of the men who fought at that level. This in turn reflected the sort of *joie de vivre* and the belief in danger and force that aligned D'Annunzio with the Futurist movement of Marinetti and with many anti-bourgeois currents in cultural and aesthetic life at the time.

As the nineteenth century drew to a close, there came a large range of thinkers and writers such as Maurice Barrès in France, such as D'Annunzio and Marinetti in Italy, who were appalled by the sterility of late nineteenth-century life and yearned for the conflicts which would engulf Europe and the world in the next century. You have a situation where each era — such as the one we're in at the moment — precedes what is coming with all sorts of conflicted and heterogeneous ideologies which only become clear once you've actually lived through the subsequent period. Between about 1880 and 1910, an enormous ferment of opinion, with men as voluble as Stalin and Hitler being in café society parts of Europe, planning what was to come or what they might be alleged to be part of at certain distant times. Men often dismissed as cranks and dreamers and wayfaring utopians on the margins of things who were destined later on to leap to the center of European culture and expectancy.

There's a great story that the French writer Jean Cocteau says about Lenin. He met a man at a party in a house in France in 1910, and the man was sitting in the house. In other words, he was looking after it while someone was away. And Cocteau said to his friends, "And who are you?" and the man said, rather portentously, "Men call me Vladimir Ilyich Ulyanov. I am known as Lenin. I am plotting the destruction of the Russian Czarist regime, and I am going to wipe out the entire ruling class in Russia and install a proletarian dictatorship." Straight out without any intermission! And they all said, "Well, that's very interesting! One applauds you, monsieur!" And he said, "What are you doing at the moment?" And he said, "I edit a small journal called *Iskra, The Spark,* which is the beginning of the ferment of the revolutionary energies which are coming to Russia and eventually the world!" And they thought, "Well, this is interesting!" You know. How many subscribers had *Iskra* got at that moment? Four hundred? Forty? Four? And yet, of course, Vladimir Ilyich Ulyanov would emerge from the chaos of post-revolutionary Russia, as Russia struggled from its defeat by the Germans in the First World War, to become the leader of the world's first sort of most toxic revolutionary state. Nothing is predictable in this life.

When the German high command sealed the Bolshevik leadership, including Vladimir Ilyich, in a train and sent it through their occupied territories into Greater Russia in the hope that it would just create more chaos and foment more distress, they had no idea that this tiny, little faction would seize maybe eleven or twelve percent in parliamentary votes and would then take over a weakened state with a small paramilitary force. Because the Bolshevik Revolution was in no sense a social revolution as its proselytizers claimed for upwards of half a century afterwards. It was an armed coup by the armed wing of a tiny political party.

There's a famous story that Lenin, Trotsky, and Stalin all slept together in one room with newspaper on the floor the day after the Revolution, and Lenin said, "Comrades! A very important thing has happened! We have been in power for one day!" And the amount of Russia that they controlled, of course, was extraordinarily small.

So, one has to realize that this ferment of ideas, Right, Left, and center, religious, aesthetic, and otherwise, occurred between 1880 and the beginning of the period that led up to the Great War and out of which most of the modern ideologies of the first half to first three-quarters of the twentieth century emerged.

D'Annunzio largely created Italian Fascism. Nearly everything that came out of the movement led by Mussolini at a later date originated with him and his ideas. The idea of the man alone, set above the people who is yet one of them, the idea of a squad of *Arditi*, of people who are passionate and fanatical and frenzied with a stiff-arm Roman salute, who are dressed in black and who are an audience for the leader, as well as security for the leader, as well as a sort of prop to make sure that the masses, particularly in the crowd, when they're listening to the leader go along with what the leader is saying, as well as a sort of nationalist chorus . . . All of these ideas come from D'Annunzio and his period of forced occupation and Italianization of the port of Fiume.

So, there's a degree to which this possible assassination attempt against D'Annunzio in 1922 which puts him out of commission for a certain period was in its way emblematic of the fact that he was a key player in Italian politics. He was the only rival for the leadership of what became known as the extreme Right with Mussolini. Certain Fascists at times looked to D'Annunzio when the fortunes of their own movement dipped.

It's noticeable that during the occupation of Fiume, which we'll come onto a bit later in this talk, D'Annunzio thought that there should be a march on Rome and rushed to align himself with the Fascists and other forces of renewal and nationalistic frenzy in Italian life after Italy's victory as part of the winning side during the Great War. That march never happened, but of course was to happen later when Mussolini and other leaders had engaged in deals with the existing Italian establishment. The Mussolinian march on power was a coup with the favor of the state it was taking over rather than a coup against the nature of the state which was hostile to what was coming. So, in a way, the Italian march was leaning on a door that was already open, and only forces like Italian Communism and so on, which are outside the circle of the state and its reference to political resources, opposed what the Mussolinians then did.

There is this view that Mussolini and the Fascist movement regularized and slightly de-romanticized the heroic conspectus of what D'Annunzio stood for. D'Annunzio was an artist, and when Fiume, which is part of Croatia, was taken over by his militia, between one thousand and three thousand strong in the early 1920s, because it had an Italian majority and he wished to secure it for Italy in relation to the post-Great War dispensation, he made music the foundation-stone of the city-state of Fiume. And there's a degree to which this is part of the extreme rhetoricism and aestheticism that D'Annunzio was into. This is not practical politics to make music your cardinal state virtue and to create idealized state assemblies with a minimum of chatter, because D'Annunzio believed not in parliamentary democracy but in a form of civics whereby each participant of the nation was represented. That's why in Fiume he begins the prospect of a corporate state, and he begins an assembly or a vouchsafe body for farmers, for workers, for employers, for the clergy, for industrialists, and so on in a manner that Mussolini would later take over, because most of what the Mussolinians did was actually pre-ordained for them by D'Annunzio's moral and aesthetic *coup d'état.*

Now, D'Annunzio believed that life should be brief and hectic and as heroic as possible, and that the Italians should be based upon the principles of the ancient Roman Empire and of the Renaissance. In other words, he quested through the Italian period of phases of thousands of years of culture for the highest possible spots upon which to base Italy in the twentieth century. At his funeral, which occurred in 1938, Mussolini declared that Italy will indeed rise to the heights of which he wished, and D'Annunzio always wanted Italy to be on the winning side and to be a major player in international and European events.

The truth of the matter, of course, is that Italy for most of its twentieth-century existence has not been a minor player, but has not been amongst the major players, has been amongst the second-tier powers of Europe in all reality, and there's a degree to which many Italian military adventures which were initiated by Mussolini fell back on German tutelage and support when they ran into difficulties, although those imperial adventures in Ethiopia and elsewhere were supported by D'Annunzio, who became very close to the regime when he realized that they wished to set up a neo-Italian empire along Romanist lines.

D'Annunzio also supported Mussolini in leaving the League of Nations, and he believed oppressed Italians who lived outside of Italy proper should be included, in an irredentist way, in Italy proper. Irredentism is the idea that if you have people of your own nationality who live outside the area of your nation-state you should incorporate them in one way or another, by conquering intermediate territory or by agglomerating them back into a larger confederation. This is the idea of having a greater country: Britain and the Greater Britain, Italy and the Greater Italy, Russia and the Greater Russia, and so forth.

There's a degree to which D'Annunzio aligned himself with the forces of conceptual modernism without being a modernist himself. In a literary and in a linguist way, he was very much a Romantic of the nineteenth-century vogue, but his sensibility was extraordinarily modern.

In contemporary Italian literature, there is no easy and defined position about D'Annunzio. One would have thought that a man who died in 1938 and his political career was over by 1922 to all effects would be historical now. D'Annunzio is still a live topic in Italy and is still controversial, not least because of the sort of Byronic "sexism" of his novels, poetry, and plays, a screenplay indeed in one case and librettos for various operas. Also, the fact that he's such a precursor of Italian Fascism to the degree that he is regarded as the first *Duce*, the first leader, the first fascistic leader of any prominence that Italy had before Mussolini, that his reputation is still extremely divisive in Italian letters. Most of the center and Left, when D'Annunzio's name is mentioned in Italy today, still go, "Ahhhh nooo!" Because he is still a figure. If you can imagine a sort of fascistic D. H. Lawrence who later had Mosley's political career up to a point, that's the nearest you get to a British example of a man like D'Annunzio. Lawrence, of course, would have a completely different reputation had he endorsed the politics of Nazi Germany in the way that he sort of endorsed, slightly, the politics of fascistic Italy. In some ways, Lawrence, who was sort of made into a cult by the Cambridge literary criticism of F. R. Leavis in Britain and I. A. Richards in the United States post-Second World War, would never have proceeded to those heights had he endorsed certain political causes of the '30s and '40s. So, in a sense, his early death was fortuitous in terms of his post-war reputation.

Robinson Jeffers, the American poet and fellow pagan with whom Lawrence communicated during his life quite manfully, fell into desuetude after the Second World War for, not advocating pro-Axis sympathy as a neutralist American, but by advocating isolationism. Isolationism is, of course, an ultra-nationalist position in American life. The belief that America should not involve itself in the teeming wars of the twentieth century, what Harry Elmer Barnes calls perpetual war for perpetual peace, but America should retreat to its own borders and only concern itself with events inside the United States of America, occasionally looking outside to the Caribbean and Latin America. But Lawrence would have gone the same way as Jeffers had he had a career like D'Annunzio and had he endorsed some of the positions that D'Annunzio did.

D'Annunzio's position on fascism outside Italy was more contradictory, because he was a nationalist first and last and ultimately it was Italy's destiny that concerned him, not that of other countries. He was in favor of leaving the United Nations, but rather like Charles Maurras in France, he was a nationalist in some ways more than a Fascist, and his nationalism was proto-fascistic even though he provided much of the aesthetic coloring for what later came in the Italian political dictatorship.

D'Annunzio was a man of great individual courage, it has to be said, and combined the ferocity of the warrior and the sensibility of the artist. One of his most famous individual coups was this seven-hundred-mile round trip in an aeroplane to drop pamphlets of a sort of pro-Western/pro-Italian type on Vienna, which is still remembered to this day. And another of his feats was attacking various German boats with small, little motor-powered launchers, something which prefigures a lot of modern warfare where great, large hulking liners and aircraft carriers can be disabled by small boats that speed around them, the principle of guerrilla type or asymmetrical warfare whereby much larger entities can be hamstrung by their smaller, Lilliputian equivalents or rivals. Again, this sort of special forces warfare in a way, whether in the air or on the sea, was part and parcel of D'Annunzio's aesthetic and ethic of life.

It's noticeable that in modern warfare, the notion of individualistic courage never goes away, but war is so much reduced to the big battalions, so much reduced to raw firepower, and so much reduced to the expenditure of force between massive units that are industrially arranged against each other that individual combat often becomes slightly meaningless. But it gravitates to certain areas: the sniper, the elite boatman or frogman, the elite warrior in the air, becomes the equivalent of the lone warrior loyal to sort of ideologies of warriorship in previous civilizations, and you can see this in the way that these men think about themselves and think about their own missions.

In a previous talk to a gathering such as this, I spoke about Yukio Mishima and the ideology of the samurai based upon the cult of *bushidō* in Japan. This is the idea of almost an aesthetic martial elitism who sees itself both in artistic and religious terms, and yet is also a morality for killing. All of these things are provided for in one package. And a man like D'Annunzio did incarnate many of these values in a purely Western and Southern European sense.

D'Annunzio's war record was such that he won most of the medals, including the gold medal, the equivalent to the Victoria Cross, and he won silver crosses which was a slightly lesser medal, and a bronze cross. He was also awarded other medals, including a British military cross, because of course he was fighting on the British and Allied side in the First [World] War.

One of his points, which was made by Mussolini and other Italian nationalists, was that Italy did not get from the First [World] War the post-war dispensation which they expected. This is true of almost everybody essentially, but it's certainly true that Italy was thrust back into the pack of secondary powers by the major victors in the First World War: Britain, and the United States, and France. Their role in the post-war peace, which of course was a highly torturous and afflictive peace upon the defeated Germany, was to have major repercussions on the decades that followed. That peace had little to do with what Italy wanted. One of the reasons for the occupation of what later became a part of Yugoslavia by paramilitary Italian arms led by D'Annunzio was his dissatisfaction with Italy's role at the table after the Great War.

His belief in "One Italy" and "Italy Forever" and "where an Italian felt injustice, Italy must be there to protect them," this belief that caused thousands of men to rise up and come to D'Annunzio's banner . . . When he began his assault on Fiume, he had about three hundred men with him. By the time it was over, he had about three thousand.

And on the Internet, you can see in 1921 enormous crowds in the city, almost everyone who's in the city is there cheering on D'Annunzio, who engaged in this increasing rhetoric from the balcony. Indeed, the Mussolinian stage scene whereby the dictator figure, or dictator *manqué* in this case, addresses the masses who look up to a balcony is all constructed and often lit up by stage lights, and that sort of thing is all part and parcel of D'Annunzionian theater. D'Annunzio would always ask the crowd rhetorical questions: "Do you love Italy?" And there's this response, "Yes!" And then there will be another response from D'Annunzio, and then there'll be another response. And if somebody gives a contrary sort of response in the crowd, because these are enormous mass meetings which are difficult to control, he has squads of men dressed in black positioned in the crowd who can sort various malefactors out. This combination of support with a degree of psychological bullying is all part of the festival of nationalistic spirit that somebody like D'Annunzio believes in building almost as a theatrical event where you let the crowd down over time by stoking them up into more and more responses, and you allow moments where the crowd just bellows and howls in response until they are replete and exhausted, and the man strides back to the edge of the balcony to begin a speech. All of these are things which Mussolini would later develop. So, D'Annunzio in a sense provides a theatrical package for what becomes Italian and Southern European radical nationalism at a later time.

He didn't live to see the full extent of Italian Fascism, but he had to be kept sweet by the Mussolinian government. Mussolini was once asked by a fellow Fascist leader in Italy what he thought of D'Annunzio and why he behaved in relation to him in the way that he did, and he said, "When you have a rotten tooth there are two solutions. You either pull it out violently or you pack it with gold, and I have decided on the secondary option with D'Annunzio." So, D'Annunzio was given a large amount of money by the Italian state to swear off political involvement after 1922, something that makes the possible assassination of him in 1922, attempted assassination, rather interesting and mysterious. No one knows whether that was an attempted assassination or not. It's quite obscure in the historical literature, but it certainly put D'Annunzio back and it put him out of commission for the entire period that the Mussolinians marched to power quite literally.

Later on, he would be awarded the leadership of the equivalent of the Royal Society of Arts; he would be awarded a state bursary which paid for a collected edition of his works that was printed and published by the Italian state itself and would be available in all libraries and schools and universities; he was awarded numerous medals and forms of honor; his house was turned into a museum which still exists and is one of the major tourist sites in contemporary Italy, where planes which he flew in the Great War are restored and can be looked at, boats which he used in the Great War are restored and can be looked at, as well as a library, a military research institute, and all sorts of photographs from the period. There is a large mausoleum to him, which is a contemporary Italian monument of significance. And he's compared in some ways to Garibaldi, the figure in the nineteenth century with his Redshirt movement that helped unite Italy as a warring, patchwork quilt of a nationality into one overall nation-state along modern lines.

D'Annunzio is one of these synthetic and syncretic figures who combine in themselves several different lives: lover, soldier, aesthete, political warrior, writer, artist. He combined four or five lives in one particular lifespan and brought together all sorts of confluences in the Italian politics of his day.

When he was elected to the Senate as an independently-minded conservative at the end of the nineteenth century, he had no real sectarian politics at all except a belief in conservatism and revolution, as he described it. He later moved across the Parliament floor to join the Left in a particular vote that broke a deadlock in Italian politics at the time, and was regarded as the creation of a new synthesis where part of the Right joined the Left and then split off again to form a different part of the Right, or could at least be said to be a precursor of those same developments.

Mussolini, of course, was sat with the socialists and was a socialist deputy, and was part of the bloc which favored nationalist rather than international solutions as part of Italian socialism. This is why during the First World War, or the run-up to it, the Axis within Italy that favored Italy's involvement in the war against strong pacifists and internationalist currents that wanted to keep Italy out of the European conflagration lost out, and one of the key proponents were the Futurists,

D'Annunzians, and proto-Fascists from the bosom of the Italian Socialist Party, who combined a degree of nationalism with quite straightforward Italian social democracy of the period.

Now, D'Annunzio married and had, I think, three children, but he was well-known for a very torrid love life consisting of a great string of mistresses. He had dalliances with two extraordinarily notorious Italian actresses, both of whom he wrote plays for and operetta. He was well regarded as a sort of *bon viveur* and a figure about whom myths constellate. Even to this day, D'Annunzio is regarded as a cad and an egotist and a scoundrel in many circles, because that is how he presented himself and the male ego in his literary works.

How original D'Annunzio was is difficult to quantify. His philosophical debt is to Nietzsche, his literary debt is to the Italian literary tradition, which essentially goes back to the Renaissance. His great use of style—he was one of the greatest stylists of the modern Italian language—has made sure that his books are in print to this day, but he still remains a controversial figure because of the politics with which he was associated.

How far and aesthetically motivated his desire for dictatorship could work in practice and would not implode because of impracticality is a moot point, but D'Annunzio certainly gave a *brio* to early Italian experimental and Right-wing politics. He gave a poetic license to authoritarianism which helped make Southern European Fascism extraordinarily culturally interesting long into the Mussolinian regime. It's interesting to notice how many writers and intellectuals aligned with the movement in Italy and made peace with its government.

Also, the use of internal oppression, which is very light-handed in Italy, was part and parcel of this doctrine of *brio* and of ubiquitousness and the use of style. In some ways it was a very style-conscious regime, an exercise in theater. Many of the post-war historians of Fascist Italy talk about it as being a sort of theatrical society with Mussolini as almost a political actor in some respects. And this is very much in the D'Annunzionian tradition which he laid down at Fiume.

At Fiume, they conquered this city which is part of Croatia but had an Italian majority at that time. The Italian governor refused to fire on D'Annunzio and his paramilitaries when they entered the city. They took it over and created a sort of corporate state within the city, heralding its creation as a city-state. They said it left the League of Nations, which they refused to recognize because Italians were being exploited by the remit of the League of Nations, the forerunner of the United Nations. They created this sort of aesthetic, fascistic junta that was part theater, part hyper-reality, and part just a governing civic administration with a military arm. And gradually, the forces of reaction, as D'Annunzio would have called them, attempted to call Fiume to account. The Allies chafed against its continued existence as an independent military satellite and city-state. Italian nationalists and others may have flocked to it, including Leftists like anarchists and syndicalists who admired D'Annunzio's *brio* and sort of cult of *machismo* and Italian irregular adventurism, which is a Medieval tradition, certainly an antique Italian tradition, with many admirers from across the spectrum. And yet in the end, the Italian state was forced to take action and fired on Fiume, and Italian naval vessels shelled the city. There was a declaration of war, somewhat absurdly, against Italy by D'Annunzio, where three thousand men took on a nation-state that could put tens of thousands of men in boats and planes into play.

Eventually, of course, when the shelling became too bad, he said he could not allow the aesthetic construction of the city to be damaged, and so he handed it over to prior Italian power and an international settlement, which involved Yugoslav control eventually came in.

But Fiume represented a direct incursion of fantasy into political life, because there is a degree to which D'Annunzio combined elements of performance art in his political vocabulary. There's no doubt that he thought of politics as a form of theater, particularly for the masses, and this is because he was an elitist, because as an elitist he partly despised the masses except as the voluntarist agencies of national consciousness. He theatricalized politics in order to give them entertainment without allowing them any particular say in what should be done. And so this idea of politics as performance art with the masses onstage but as an audience, an audience that responded and yet was not in charge, because there's nothing democratic about D'Annunzio from his individualistic egotism as an artist all the way through to his sort of quasi-dictatorship of Fiume. So he represented a particularly pure synthesis, and the violence that was used and so on was largely rhetorical, largely staged, largely a performance, partly a sort of theater piece.

In postmodernism, there's this idea that artists crash cars, burn buildings, and exhibit what they've done in gallery spaces and that sort of thing as an attempt at an incursion of reality into the artistic space. And D'Annunzio did it the other way around. There was a sort of incursion not of reality into the artistic space, but of artistry into the political space, and he went seamlessly from writing these novels of male chauvinism and excess and erotic predatoriness and Italianate *brio* to running a city-state, almost without any sort of marked gap between the two moments. And in the chaotic situation of post-Great War Italy and its environs, he found a template upon which his dreams—his critics would say his bombastic dreams—could be lived out, and there is a sort of dreamer of the day element to D'Annunzio, but he was also quite hard-headed and practical, and most of his political exercises in chauvinism came off, unlike many dreams that remain in the scrap-heap of political alternatives.

So, in a sense, D'Annunzio's greatest novel was the creation of what became the Italian Fascist state, which until it was defeated externally and internally was one of the most stable societies modern Europe has seen.

So, this belief in a nation's ability to renew itself by bringing various tendencies that are abroad within it together and synthesizing them through the will of one man who must be a visionary of one sort or another is part and parcel of D'Annunzio's legacy. It's why he can't settle down and just be an artist. It's why, indeed, his post-war Italian reputation is so mixed, because he can't be divorced from the politician and the statesman that he indeed was.

It's interesting to think of how the world would have developed if European nationalities would have increasingly fallen under the sway of these cross-bred artistic, hybridized figures. Nearly all far Right, and some far Left, leaders have these sorts of characteristics: extreme individuality, colorful backgrounds in the past, a sort of anti-bourgeois sentiment, a refusal to live a conventional life completely, the belief in new forms, and the construction of new forms of modernity almost in a haphazard and experimental way. These people only get their chance during war, economic breakdown, chaos, and revolutionary change when everything comes up for grabs, and there is a new dispensation abroad. But it is noticeable that these people do get their chance when these events occur.

It's also noticeable that the post-war period, very much in Western Europe at any rate, is dominated by two factors. One is the Cold War, which congeals the Continent into two rival blocs, and the other under partial American domination in the Western sector and direct Soviet domination, of course, of the Eastern bloc, but the second is a fear of contamination through change which is underpinned by the desire to keep market economies functioning at a tolerable level of sufficiency. It's quite obvious that there is a terror abroad in the Western liberal landscape about what would occur if there is an economic collapse. Not just a slow-down, not just a depression or recession or series of recessions that ends in a Japanese-like depression which can go on for twenty years where you don't grow at all, zero growth, but something much more devastating than that. An actual crack and crash in the system itself. Because with mass democracy, there is no knowing what sorts of demagogues and what sorts of visionaries people might start voting for in small or larger numbers when such a crash occurs and when they literally can't pay their bills, and so D'Annunzio came out of an era of chronic instability and fashioned that instability to his own liking and making, because Fiume was the prototype for a state.

Indeed, in ancient Southern Europe, the city-state was the forerunner of the nation-state. He was attempting to do with an Athens or a Sparta of his own imagination and will and intellect what later became Mussolinian Italy on a nation-wide scale, and if Italy had succeeded in carving out an empire for itself in North Africa and further afield in modernity, it would have been the basis for an Italian empire, because the nature of these things is to expand. That type of power always chafes against the possibility of restriction, and unless it comes up against a greater external force, will always chafe against it in an attempt to push it back and gain greater suzerainty thereby. That's inevitable. Even under mercantilist pressure, the British Empire adopted that sort of course for many centuries until, if you like, the stabilization of the twentieth century and the loss of empire in mid-century.

So one will see, if there are enormous economic crashes in the near to distant future, the sort of politics that D'Annunzio represented come back. No one knows what form it will take because things never repeat themselves. They only seem to, because the syntheses that are created are always new and always original. But this crossover between theater, literature, lived demagoguery, the martial and martinet spirit, and the spirit of the lone adventurer, the spirit of the marauder, the spirit of the armed troubadour is very much a part and parcel of what D'Annunzio stood for. And his present notoriety in contemporary Italy is because he is a man of so many parts and such a threatening overall presence — threatening in the sense that Italian Fascism, although much more integrated into the historical story than fascisms elsewhere, is still very much a devilish shadow cast over the post-Italian polity that all are aware of and yet few dare to speak of with any courage or glory.

D'Annunzio believed that courage and glory and heroic belief in national affirmation were the very principles of life. And his example, so out of kilter with contemporary reality, is interesting and refreshing. D'Annunzio is like a sort of Julius Caesar crossed with Jack London. There's a strange amalgam of tendencies living out of one man, and it's remarkable that he could bring that union or fusion of with such panache and charisma. Probably it was the military career that he had during the Great War that enabled him to step out of the literary study and into the statesman's counting house, onto the statesman's balcony. Without that experience in the Great War, I doubt he would have had the following to achieve that. But D'Annunzio represents this strange amalgam in European man of the restless adventurer and the poet, of the dreamer and the activist, of the stoic and the fanatic.

The city-state that he created at Fiume provided for religious toleration and atheism, because of course as a Nietzschean, D'Annunzio was an atheist and was not religiously motivated, even though the paganism of his literature harks back to the neo-paganism of the Renaissance and to the Roman Empire of Antiquity.

The real source of origin for D'Annunzio's moral equipment has to be ancient Rome, and as I look about me in this society, there are an enormous number of novels, aren't there, devoted to ancient Rome? Quite populist, mainstream fare. And it's quite clear that there is a fascination with Europe's past and with its authoritarian, bellicose, adventurist, and escapist past, and possibly through the mirror image of intermediaries like D'Annunzio there may be a link to a new and a more invigorating Europe of adventure and of skill and of destiny and of the will of the desperado and of the man who will never take no for an answer and of the man who would chant these slogans that Achilles uses in Homeric epics to the crowd and hear the *Arditi* chant them back again, and that these are echoes which you can still hear and which are still not entirely dormant in Europe at the present time, as the Balkan Wars of the 1990s proved in their bloody way. And there's a degree to which these prior giants of Europe are sleeping, but are not at rest, and there is always the fear in contemporary liberal establishments that these figures and the forces that they represented will be catalyzed yet again in the future by new visionaries and by new leaders and by new literati and by new sources of inspiration who combine the individual and the collective, combine the national and the quietude of the man alone and combine the Renaissance and the ancient world in a new pedigree of what it means to be a man, what it means to be a European, and what it means to have a destiny in the modern world.

D'Annunzio preconfigured much of European history until at least the late 1940s, which bearing in mind he was born towards the middle of the nineteenth century was quite an achievement. It is not to say that figures who are alive now are in themselves creating the synthesis for forces that will emerge in the next fifty years.

Thank you very much!

CHARLES MAURRAS &
ACTION FRANÇAISE*

Now, *French Action* was largely a newspaper, but it extended out into a political movement between the First and Second World Wars, and to a certain extent the second decade of the twentieth century just passed, so after the first of those two wars. What made Action Française so special was the theoretical and literary contribution of Charles Maurras.

Now, Maurras was born in Provence. He was an intellectual who was drawn to a kind of revolutionary tradition in French life. France had always been characterized until the later nineteenth century by a significant quadrant of the population who rejected the logic of the French Revolution. The French Revolution, which lasted from 1789 until Napoleon's essential conquest of military power in the French Republic in 1796 and his full dictatorship in 1799 thereafter to 1815, was a period of extraordinary and grotesque change the likes of which European civilization had not seen before. Considerable parts of France, like the Vendée and elsewhere, also fought against the revolutionary tyranny of that time. These were known as the Whites, or the counter-revolutionaries. This tradition of regretting the French Revolution was part of High Catholicism and part of the deep social conservatism of sections of the bourgeoisie that existed in France throughout the existence of the Third Republic.

The Third Republic was created after the collapse of France's military honor in 1870 when the Prussians badly defeated France in the territorial war between two major European states. The emergence and unification of Prussia on the disemboweled and disinherited torso of modern France was something the French took very much to heart. Particularly in

---

* This was Jonathan Bowden's last lecture, delivered at The London Forum on March 24, 2012, just five days prior to his sudden death. The transcript was made by V. S.

1871, there was a Communistic rising in Paris known as the Commune which started in a particular period and which French troops put down in an extremely bloody and savage way with the sponsorship of German arms behind them in the rear.

Now, Maurras believed totally in what he called "integral nationalism" or *nationalisme intégral*. This is the idea that France came first in all things. Regarded as a "Germanophobe" for most of his life, Maurras escaped death after the Second World War during the period of purification, when a large number of politicians, collaborators, Vichyites, revisionists, quasi-revisionists, independently minded Right-wing intellectuals, and many people who fought in the Middle East and were involved in some way or another with the Vichy regime were put to death or were hounded from the society. The trial that Maurras had at this particular time was truncated and was laughable in terms of French statute then or since.

The Resistance was very much enamored with the prospect of guillotining Maurras, seeing him as the spiritual father of Vichy. However, there was a degree to which this was an incorrect assessment, because de Gaulle had sat at Maurras' feet during much of his early life. The interesting thing about Maurras is that he did not just influence the French radical Right, he influenced the entire French Right and he provided all of the families of the French Right, particularly those who looked to a more Orléanist monarchical replacement, those who looked to a Bourbon monarchical replacement (this is the Republic, of course), those who looked to a Napoleonic claim, and those that wanted a different type of Right-wing repub-lic — all found in Maurras' theories sustenance for the soul.

Maurras was released from prison into a hospital in the early 1950s and died soon after. He died in a degree of disgrace, and yet there's also a degree to which that disgrace was not complete, nor did it totally fill the sky. Maurras was removed from the Académie Française, the French Academy, which is the elixir of conservative and reactional and literalist and neo-Classical standings in French intellectual life, yet he was re-posed by somebody who was almost identical to him given the aged and conservative conspectus of the Academy.

There is a degree to which Maurras identified four enemies of the French nation as he perceived them from early on in his political career and before the creation of the Action Française movement, which was an anti-democratic movement and which never took part in parliamentary elections. We shall come on to the view that politics was primary for Maurras, unlike spirituality and religion, in a moment.

Maurras believed that these four "anti-nations" within France were Protestants, Jews, Masons, and all foreigners living on French territory. He perceived all of France as essentially sacred and universal in expectancy and energy. He believed that the Third Republic was a rotten, bourgeois counterpace that needed to be ripped down and replaced by absolutist, legitimist, and monarchical tendencies. Unlike the post-war radical Right in France which has made peace with the Republic for reasons of electoral viability, such as the Front National for example which never even intimates that it would like to restore the monarchy if it were ever put anywhere near power, Maurras and his associates were obsessed with monarchical restoration. This gave their type of Rightism a deeply reactionary and deeply counter-revolutionary cast of thought, but it is important to realize that these things were significantly popular in large areas of French national life. Large areas of the unassimilated aristocracy, the upper middle class, most of the upper class, and even parts of the essentially middle bourgeoisie retained a suspicion of the legacy of the French Revolution and wished to see the recomposition of France along monarchical lines. These policies even lasted well into the twentieth century, even beyond the Second World War. Even into the 1960s a better part of five percent of the French nation rejected the logic of the French Revolution, which is a quite extraordinary number of people given the fact that the revolutionary inheritance had lasted so long and had been re-imposed upon the country after the revolutions, themselves abortive, in 1848.

Maurras believed that France needed a strong and social Catholicism in order to be viable. This is complicated given his own tendentious hold on religious belief. Maurras, although never an atheist, rejected the early, comforting Catholicism of his childhood and youth and was an agnostic for most of his life. This did not prevent him from adopting a viewpoint which was fundamentalist in relation to Catholic rigor and in the belief of what would now be called traditionalist Catholicism since the Vatican II settlement of the early 1960s, which in Catholic terms began to liberalize the Church and adapted it to a modern, secular age inside of France and beyond its borders.

Maurras believed that spirituality was intensely important for a people and without it a people rotted and became as nothing. He therefore supported radical religion as a maximalizing social agenda whilst not believing in it himself. Indeed, he implicitly distrusted much of the Gospel message and found the Old Testament disastrous in its pharisaical illumination.

Maurras believed that Christianity was a useful tool that an elite would make use of in order to create a docile, happy, contented, and organic society. This means that the Papacy was deeply suspicious of Maurras despite the fact that politically he seemed to be a drummer boy for what they might have been perceived to want. This led to the prorogation of the Action Française movement by the Vatican at a particular time. I believe this occurred in the 1920s and was not rescinded until 1939, by which time Maurras had been elected to the Académie Française. The Vatican was concerned at the agnosticism from the top and the synthetic use of Catholicism as a masking agent and cloaking ideology for Right-wing politics inside France that it otherwise found quite a lot to support in. There were enormous numbers of clergy in the Action Française as a movement, and they were shocked and horrified by the removal of Papal support which undercut support for the Action Française from key sectors of French life at a particular time.

Maurras believed in anti-Semitism as a core element of his ideology and beliefs. He believed that Jews should have no part or role in national life and no role whatsoever in the sort of France which he wished to see. Although they had not been responsible in any sort of way for much of the events of the French Revolution, he believed that their emancipation, as the emancipation had occurred in Germany, Britain, and elsewhere during the nineteenth century, had led to a collusion of interests which were detrimental to the sacred nature of France.

He was also strongly anti-Protestant and anti-Masonic and had a view of nationality which is regarded almost as simpleminded today. He basically thought that to command a status inside the French nation you had to be French in word, in deed, and in prior cultural inheritance. It wasn't any good to claim that you were French. You had to be French in terms of the self-limiting definitions of what it was to be national. This meant that there were radiating hierarchies within France, as within other European societies inside modernity. This was the idea that some people were more French than others and this implicit elitism was always part and parcel of the nature of his movement.

It's important to realize that there was an intellectual complexity about French Action which commands a considerable degree of respect, especially from a distance. *French Action* appealed to an enormous number of intellectuals across the spectrum even though it was sold by quasi-paramilitaries in the streets. The youth wing and the radical wings of the Action Française movement were known as the Knights of the King, or Camelots du Roi, and they sold these publications in the streets, often engaging in ferocious fights with Left-wing street gangs who attempted to crowd the same pitches, particularly in Montmartre in the center of Paris and the center of other urban areas.

Maurras believed in action in the streets as a part of politics and disprivileged voting, which he thought was sterile, bourgeois, majoritarian, and anti-elitist. One wonders if there was ever a coherent structure to come to power in the Action Française movement, and the only way in which this can be corralled with all the historical evidence is to see the Action Française as a [inaudible] group for a particular type of restorationist, social conservatism, and Catholicism inside France.

If Maurras' vision had been successful, you would have had a national France with an extremely strong and powerful monarchy and an extremely strong and powerful, even hermetic Catholic clergy, at the heart of the nation. You would have had strong military and other institutions that ramify with these other elements of traditional French power as expressed in Bourbon restorationist and pre-revolutionary and post-revolutionary Romantic, royalist France.

Maurras believed that to be happy, people had to be content in the structures of their own livery and their own inheritance. The inheritance of the French nation was all-important, and this is why he collaborated with Third Republic politicians such as General Boulanger towards the end of the nineteenth century. He did this in order to undermine the nature of the liberal republic and lead to reforms and authoritarian constitutions within it which would have served his purpose. He supported a large range of bourgeois, radical, and liberal politicians at the time of the First World War, which he thought was a national surprise of glory and a chance for France to redeem herself on the battlefield against a traditional enemy, which he always perceived as Germany.

This is the area where Maurras is most disprivileged by contemporary nationalist thinkers across Europe and even beyond. His obsession with Germany and with Germany's strength and his belief that France was belittled by any strength in Germany led him to support French arms in both the First World War, 1914 to '18, and the Second World War, '39 to '45. Initially, he supported de Gaulle and de Gaulle's use of tank warfare in the early stages of the Second World War. Of course, by the time de Gaulle became supreme commander of French forces, France would be decimated on the battlefield and there was nothing left to repair or even to defend. Guderian, who had read all of the theory which de Gaulle had based his own warfare predictions upon, had already trumped that particular card, and the Germans used British and French ideas about tank warfare to defeat both the British Expeditionary Force and the French army in France. Seizing with revolutionary energy the generational gap in the conduct of warfare, the Germans routed and humiliated the French, who had fought them to a standstill in the past in the Great War, within a matter of weeks, by maneuvering around the Maginot Line and by passing through the allegedly impassable Ardennes Forest to appear behind French lines with roving and energetic Panzer squadrons backed by Stuka bombers.

This collapse and catastrophe became a divine and a national surprise to Maurras. Maurras never actively collaborated, although nearly all those in his circle would find themselves involved in the Vichy government at one time or another. Vichy began an institutionalization of a revolution from above and a national revolution within France largely permitted under German auspices, particularly in the early years before the radicalization and momentum-building of what became the French Resistance under British SOE [Special Operations Executive] and the Gaullist movement in opposition and exile.

Maurras believed that the only true purpose of a Frenchman was to enhance the glory of France, and all other was tackle and blither. He believed that during the German occupation, it was best for French ideologues such as themselves to retreat to his family estate and live there in quietude, even though many of his philosophical children collaborated openly with German arms both within and beyond Vichy. People like Laval and Déat with his neo-socialist movement, and people like the founder of the French Popular Party, Doriot, the Parti Populaire Français (PPF), all collaborated in various degrees or were influenced by an attraction or repulsion to Maurras' ideas in one form or another. He was truly the great old man of the French Right by this time.

After the war, the resistance sought to blame Maurras for much of the collaboration which had gone on, including the expulsion of some Jews from France, the international humiliation, as they perceived it, of French subjection to German arms, and the neo-colonial aspects within Europe of German policy in the French nation-state. It's true to point out, however, that German military rule in France was surprisingly liberal and even benign in comparison to the full-on fury that could be exercised elsewhere in accordance with radical ideologies that had little to do with the calm, cultural intensity when Colonel Abetz met Robert Brasillach for coffee and croissants in a bar in Paris during the French occupation. There was intense collaboration between the young, former students of Maurras like

Brasillach, who edited a fascist magazine called *Je suis partout* which means "I am everywhere," and cultural Germans such as Abetz who were part and parcel of the German regime that had been installed over Vichy and to one side of it to allow Right-wing Frenchmen to run their own country, albeit under German auspices. The relationship was probably somewhat similar to the relationship of American imperialism has with client states in the Third World, such as Karzai's regime in Afghanistan, which controls Afghanistan and is ultimately beholden to American power, or what remains, in that particular society.

Maurras wasn't guillotined after the war because he significantly told at his trial, "Nobody hates the Germans more than me." And this is what saved him from the guillotine, because the Resistance, although they were dying to guillotine him and would have given their eyes and teeth for it, couldn't do so because this gnarled, knotty Frenchman was irreducible on that particular point. So, they gave him life imprisonment instead which, as an old man, was effectively a death sentence in and of itself. When it was read out to him in the court, a steaming Maurras leapt to his feet and declared, "It is the revenge of Dreyfus!" An otherwise obscure reference, which for those who are culturally knowledgeable about the entire extensive life of Maurras would have realized refers to the Dreyfus case at the end of the nineteenth century.

This is again an important disjunction between Maurras and much of the rest of the Right. Maurras was not concerned whether Dreyfus was guilty or not of passing secrets and engaging in espionage, of helping a foreign power, and so on. What he was concerned with is the dishonor done to the French judiciary if he was not found guilty and done to the French army and national and state society if he was about to get away with this. This idea that an individual could be found guilty for connective and social-organic reasons irrespective of his actual innocence of an offense one-to-one and in the customary nature of normal life is anathema to liberal ideas of the sovereignty of the individual that should be placed in a premium position in relation to all social actions.

Maurras was a fundamentalist anti-Dreyfusard and was part of a campaign spearheaded by elements of the revanchist Catholic Church and post-Boulanger elements in the French Republic to the extent that Dreyfus should be found guilty and executed if possible. For many like Maurras, the actual condemnation of Dreyfus which ensued and his being sent to Devil's Island in the Caribbean was a minor punishment in comparison to the ingloriousness of the episode for France and what it told you about the conduct of the French national general staff at that time.

The Dreyfus case divided France between brother and brother, between father and children, between man and wife like no other case that had convulsed the nation in the course of its late nineteenth-century/early twentieth-century development. It was truly one of those instances which define a generation. When Zola wrote *J'accuse . . . !* and accused the French police, army, and courts of essentially fixing on an unfortunate man and blaming him for the sins of others and deporting him to Devil's Island as a result of a false charge, he laid an explosive mound at the bottom of French national life which men like Maurras were determined to defuse.

Maurras believed that the English were always perfidious and were always against the divine France, although there were moments when he sought collaboration with English and British figures, but always against the more dreaded bogey of Germany. It an be seen from a distance that Maurras' nationalism has negative and anti-European features, although its simplicity and its purity about who belongs and who doesn't belong is very clear and is easy to sustain. His views were not particularly racial beyond the fact that France was the leading light of world civilization and had to be treated as such. It was quite clear what he meant by who he was and who he was not, a Frenchman or a Frenchwoman, in the era in which he lived. You inherited genealogically what you were from the generations that had lived in the society prior to you and you were a Catholic and you were, to all intents and purposes, a reasonably pious one and you yearned for the return of the monarchy in France as against the secular republican institutions which replaced the monarchical structures of the Bourbon era after the Revolution, and again after the Restoration which followed after the Revolution. And you were not Protestant and you were not a Mason and you were not a Jew and you were not a foreigner and you were not of foreign mixture, namely of non-national French admixture. These things are quite clear and quite capacious in their reasonableness.

There's a degree to which Maurras' intense nationalism has fueled an enormous amount of the radical Right that exists in the south of Europe and the southeast of Europe and further in Central and Latin America, where his ideas have been taken to heart by many Dominican, Costa Rican, Brazilian, and Argentinian nationalist writers and thinkers and academics. His thinking is also most crucial to the development of Catholic societies and, of course, he has little social interplay with the Anglo-Saxon world. Maurras seems to have little to say to Anglo-Saxony, though much to say to the integral nature of the nation which is always the divine and unyielding France.

Where did Maurras get his opinions from? A strong bourgeois background and an affiliation with the French provinces led to an identification with the rural ideal of France as a place touched by the glory of God, even a deity that he didn't subscribe to for much of his active life. Maurras believed that France had a new destiny amongst all of the nations on Earth not to bring people together, not to supervise people, and not to be loyal to Swiss institutional ideas, as he dismissed the ideas of Rousseau, who was Swiss and strongly influenced by Calvinist and Protestant thinking, which he blamed for the French Revolution.

Rousseau once declared in the first line of his *Social Contract* that in the prisons of the future, men will have liberty, *libertas*, stamped upon their chains. This is a uniquely Protestant idea whereby even the social organs of correction are there to free the individual from bondage. It's a notable incident that in Louisiana, in the southern state of the United States, the steel batons that American police use for riot control have "liberty" inscribed upon the baton. This means that there's the head of a rioter is literally broken by a riot policeman. You are being beaten over the head with freedom. You are being beaten into freedom! And this uniquely, sort of sadomasochistic and ultra-Protestant view whereby you are being punished in freedom, for freedom, by freedom is a uniquely American take upon the French Revolution. Indeed, handcuffs wielded by many American police forces have "freedom" written upon them. So, as you are handcuffed and beaten, you are receiving both liberty and freedom. And these are very important ideas which come from the French Revolution.

When you stand before a French court, you have to prove your innocence. As everybody knows, the British idea, which transcends the Atlantic and is visible in the jurisprudence of the United States, is that you are innocent before the bar of the courts and you have various barristers there to defend your right. In France, the opposite is true, in accordance with revolutionary jurisprudence. The state knows best. The state has divulged religiosity to itself. The state is the residual legatee of all ideas of liberty and dispassionate justice. You have to prove your innocence to the state, because if the state argues in a prior way for the possibility of your guilt, you must be guilty of something, or why else would the state dare to accuse you?

Maurras' ideas come quite close to certain Anglo-Saxon ideas in his rejection of this idea of the martial, republican, and even Protestant French republican state. This means that Maurras seeks help from German and English intellectual critics even as he is unmasking French intellectual culture for its support of and tolerance of the French Revolution.

The French Revolution remains the most cardinal event in history as regards the modern history of France. The French Revolution characterized an enormous range of change in European society and in the lifestyle of European man. If you remember, the Revolution had quite timid beginnings with the desire for bourgeois reformism and the integration of politicians like Mirabeau in 1789. It then morphed into a more legalistic liberal assembly with a legislative assembly in 1790-1791 which then became the much more revolutionary Convention in 1792, '93, and '94. This is the period associated with the Terror and the dominion of Maximilien Robespierre. Robespierre had his rival, Danton, who he sent successfully to the guillotine, but he only preceded him by a matter of a few months, was convulsed by the idea that he was imposing with revolutionary violence the implementation of justice upon France and that he'd been given the right to do so not by God, but by a new-fangled Deist cult or religion called the Cult of the Supreme Being. This attempt is the height of the Revolution's attempt to replace Catholicism with an atheistic cult, whereby reason was worshipped as a goddess and a naked virgin was placed in the Tricolor with a liberty cap on the high altar in Notre Dame by French revolutionary Jacobins, deeply shocked the sensibility of Catholic France that it had never forgiven Paris for its revolutionary energies which were disliked by much of the rest of society.

For much of French history, Paris had always been the center of revolution, even though the French revolutionary anthem, "La Marseillaise," comes from the revolutionary National Guard, who walked from Marseille to Paris in order to save revolutionary Paris by adding fuel from the most revolutionary and violent part of the provinces who were then fighting against the Whites, or the counter-revolutionaries, as they came to be known.

Napoleon Bonaparte was an equivocal figure for Maurras. He liked the authoritarianism, he liked the glorification of France, but he also saw the extension of French imperialism under Bonaparte's agency to be anti-French and to ultimately portend to national dishonor. This meant that there was, if not a pacifism, then a limit to national aggrandizement in Maurras' scheme of things. If the nation was crucial to all social development, the nation had borders, and the nation had limits, and authoritarianism inevitably put constraints upon social action, which reminds people that Maurras remains a sort of radical or revolutionary conservative.

Regarded retrospectively as something of a French fascist, Maurras was never fascistic, although his conservativism contained strongly sublimated elements of fascism and quasi-fascism and certain beliefs in the corporate state and certain methodological axes which he would share with movements in

Salazar's Portugal, Mussolini's Italy, and Franco's Spain. All of these three regimes were endorsed by Maurras and by the Action Française. Hitler's movement in Germany and its successful breakthrough there was in no sense endorsed. Indeed, he supported de Gaulle, and he supported mainstream Third Republican politicians who were anti-Hitler just as he supported Clemenceau in the First World War because he was anti-Kaiser.

The threat to France from Germany and the helplessness of France in the face of German military might were abiding themes for Maurras, who saw the possibility of defeat on the battlefield as a moral and spiritual defeat for France, although like all quixotic and intuitive nationalists, Maurras believed that France could never be totally defeated. A political system had gone down under the Panzers, a political system had gone down under the Stuka bombers, but France itself was irrational and eternal and would always spring up again.

Initially, he supported the de Gaullist fight against the Germans. He immediately switched to Vichy and national liberation when he saw that much of what he wanted in policy terms could be instituted under German aegis. The fact that it was under German aegis caused him great psychic pain and wanton disregard. He therefore retreated to his own estates to cover the dichotomy of supporting Vichy at a distance without wishing to be seen to champion its German precursor.

Maurras lived in an era of tumultuous change and violent excess, none more so than the events of the sixth of February 1934. These events, unlike the Paris events of 1968, which have been sort of emblazoned in world history and have counterparts in Berkeley, California and the streets of Britain and the streets of West Germany as it then was and elsewhere throughout the Western world, the events of 1934 have largely been forgotten and have been deliberately dropped down the memory hole, collectively and historically. Maurras, however, was deeply involved in the events of 1934, which were nothing more or less than an attempt to overthrow the French Third Republic by revolution from the Right wing.

Riddled with scandal and approximating to extreme decay due to the economic lashings of Depression from the United

States and elsewhere who were beginning to humiliate the French exchequer, the radical Right decided to depose by going onto the streets of the French Third Republic in early February 1934. This was awful rioting, and it was very serious and very destructive social rioting by about one hundred thousand demonstrators from all of the French combat action leagues that then existed in the country. These included the Action Française, they included the large veteran association from the First World War called Cross of Fire, or Croix-de-Feu. It also involved large apolitical veterans' organizations and smaller, more targeted Right-wing combat veterans' leagues.

All of these movements marched on Paris and marched on the National Assembly and marched on the presidential buildings in an attempt to overthrow the Third Republic with violent revolutionary activism from the streets. It's quite remarkable that these events have been excised from history to the degree that they have, particularly as they forced a catalytic change in French political life. Daladier's regime, which was part of a Left front and Left coalition government, collapsed and was replaced by the more general government of the Right.

One of the interesting examples of this period is the fact that, unlike today, where the radical Right is shunted off to the side and all the areas of political thought including the moderate Right strive to have nothing to do with it whatsoever, in that era the radical Right infused the mainstream Right and even liberal, center-Right elements of the Right were not immune to radical Right-wing ideas. This shows you that politics is about energy and it's about how you corral and contrast various forms of energy over time. There is no earthly reason why radical forms of opinion, as occurred in the '60s the other way around on the Left, cannot influence more moderate, more statist, more staid, and more centric forms of opinion. It all depends upon the timing, the character of the men involved, and the secondary forces which they can put into play. No one knew this better than Maurras, who influenced these structured, highly controlled Right-wing mobs, which is what they essentially amounted to, in their assaults on French liberal bourgeois power at this time.

Sixteen died as a result of the rioting, and over two thousand were injured, which is a large number of injuries to be sustained in endless fighting with French riot police and French police who turned out *en masse* to defend the Third Republic. Communists and socialists and trade unionists of the Left also mobilized large counter-demonstrations. Very much akin to events which occurred in Dublin at not too distant a period, when there was a concertedly disconcerted attempt by the Civic Guard movement of Eoin O'Duffy to overthrow the post-IRA Fianna Fáil movement which then dominated the Irish Republic. It should be noticed that both societies had a penchant for political violence and for the rhetoric of extremism in the street, and both were Roman Catholic societies, unlike Britain, which existed of course halfway between these two polities.

The Right failed in both Ireland and France to replicate what had occurred in Portugal, Spain, and Italy, never mind Germany. However, the radical Right had an enormous transforming impact upon the entire Right wing, which led a large element of the pre-collaborationist cabinet in the mid- to late-1930s to collaborate once the Vichy government was set up.

Vichy is always described as a regime by historians in an attempt to discredit it in relation to a proper government which is so described. Yet there is a degree to which the Vichy government had the support actively of at least a third of the French. De Gaulle, through a remarkable piece of political legerdemain after the war, said that no one ever collaborated. This is after the purification, of course, which killed many thousands of those who were alleged to have done so. But the trick of saying that no one collaborated allowed the post-war generations to unite over the fact that there was a German occupation, no French collaboration except for a few purists and traitors, and a Resistance movement activated from home and abroad. It was a clever, intellectual, and ideological start to enable France to recover more quickly after the war and to settle these differences without being too hawkish or squeamish about it. But there is a degree to which it was a lie and a blatant untruth.

France bore quite a large price for its staunching of social peace after 1945. You have to remember that after 1945 there was no effective Right in France, because the whole of the Right had been allegedly discredited by collaboration. This meant that there was an enormous gap and only classic centrist, conservative movements fielded candidates against the center and Left in the immediate post-war elections.

De Gaulle, of course, was trying to triumphally capture the market for existing Right-wing opinion with his Mouvement républicain populaire (MRP). De Gaulle had subliminally fascistic credentials for some of his politics and also went back to yearnings for a hard man and a strong man to govern France with an iron hand. These go back to General Boulanger and back to the Bonapartism of the nineteenth century. De Gaulle's movement, with his endless personality cult and military drills and obsession with the cult of the leader, certainly had strong fringe associations with the radical Right which he'd nevertheless repudiated and excoriated, both in action and in print.

No internal warfare on the Right has been more striking than the one in France between the legacy of de Gaullist historical tradition and the legacy of collaboration. This again is to be seen in the Algerian War long after Maurras' death in which the two wings of the French Right fight fanatically with each other. The government and the Civic Action Service movement and the Barbouzes fighting with the official French army against both the Algerian nationalists of the FLN and the ultra-Right-wing Secret Army Organization, or Organisation de l'armée secrete, which was formed by revolutionary members of the paratroopers and other French regiments firstly in Indo-China and then in Algeria to prevent the removal of Algeria from the French nation.

France and Algeria, of course, were joined at the hip in accordance with the Napoleonic doctrine of *Algérie française*. In the end, the division had to occur, but at least a million French Algerians, who were totally French of course, *colons, pieds noirs*, blackfeet, came back from North Africa to live in the south of France, where they became the bedrock for the Front National vote in the deep south of the country in generations to come.

There is also a degree to which Maurras' influence on the French Right is pervasive, and this is the influence of social Catholicism. At every large FN event there is a feverous mass. For those not in the know, this is a traditionalist type of Catholicism that rejects Vatican II and settlements around it in the contemporary Catholic Church. It essentially is an old-fashioned, in Protestant terms, smells and bells mass whereby the priest turns hieratically to God and doesn't look at the congregation, and the congregation look at him, or look at his back, and he's looking up because he's looking up at that which is exalted and beyond him. This type of social Catholicism which exists in the FN on a take-it-or-leave-it basis, because if you don't believe in it you don't have to go along with it, it's part and parcel of their appeal to all of those national constituencies which were not buried in 1945 and were not buried in 1789 and were not buried in 1815, but have continued to exist as a vital part of the French nation and of the French national whole.

Maurras' belief in the integral France—organic, unified, militarized, Catholicized, and hierarchical—was never achieved during his lifetime, but his influence on the French Right-wing and on neo-Bourbon, legitimist, Orléanist, and Bonapartist tendencies of opinion was profound. His influence on French military thinking was also profound, although his influence on Catholicism became strained when Catholic humanists like Jacques Maritain, who had been close to the Action Française for a considerable period, moved away from it in the 1920s. The Papacy moved against Maurras and the Action Française because of his doctrine of politics first. Maurras believed that if politics were put first, all the other problems that beset France and led to spiritual difficulties could be changed retrospectively.

However, there was a degree to which this put the cart partly before the horse. By making himself a declared agnostic and by being relatively open about this fact, he played into the hands of certain radical Catholic traditionalists who didn't like a mass movement that used Catholicism synthetically to cover over political differences of opinion inside France.

He was also guilty of the anti-legitimist claim put forward by many deeply conservative apolitical and asocial French

Catholics. This was the view that they should have nothing to do with the bourgeois Third Republic and that they should remain French and Catholic forever irrespective of a wicked regime that could not be stopped from sinning in its own right. Maurras would have nothing to do with this and believed that politics first, second, and third was necessary for the redemption of France.

The idea of monarchical restoration and a return of the French monarchy was not a quaint political ideal as far as Maurras and his immediate supporters were concerned. They believed that only by repudiating the Republic, only by ripping out the accretions of what could be described as the French version of the Bolshevik regime, namely the latter-day inheritance of the French republican, revolutionary tradition and all of its structures, could the France that he wanted be brought about.

Although post-war forms of the radical Right-wing in France have had to make peace with republicanism in order to survive and to contest democratic elections where they have had considerable support, more so than in most other Western European countries, there is a degree to which Maurras was quite technically direct in the issue of the French republican experiment and the mass terror that it induced between 1792 and 1794, which cast the shadow of a guillotine across French revolutionary rhetoric.

Most of the great Right-wing figures, such as Abel Bonnard, look back through Maurras to the great ultramontanist figure of Joseph de Maistre. Joseph de Maistre, who wrote in the late eighteenth century and earlier, is responsible for the doctrine of Papal infallibility up to a point, at least in terms of its theoretical mark when it was introduced quite late in the day in 1870 in recognition to extra-Catholic and intra-Catholic disputes.

Maurras was determined to see Catholicism revived within France and put at the heart of the French nation, and he did residually return to the Catholicism of his childhood near to his own deathbed. Whether this was just an insurance policy or was a genuine conversion to the faith with which he had always lingered is open for his biographers to contest.

Maurras was a peppery individual with a sort of reynardical moustache and trimmed beard. He was splenetic and outrageous in debate and commentary. He called for the assassination of many public figures from the editorial mouthpiece of his magazine, for which he was given many suspended sentences. When a French politician argued that all of the Right-wing combat leagues should be disarmed in France because he saw the danger of the events of 1934, Maurras called for his assassination in print, which is the calling for an execution of a government minister. He was jailed for eight months for this transgression.

Maurras was never afraid to speak his mind about any of the problems that beset France, from the Dreyfus case through to the conduct of the French armies in the First World War to the conduct of the Treaty of Versailles. He also wanted France to impose more rigorous and more judgmental and more harsh and caustic sanctions on Germany, long considered by most Western historians to be a disastrous maneuver. But there is nothing in relation to what it is to be French beyond which Charles Maurras would not go.

Maurras saw himself as the quiet leader of a counter-revolutionary force in French life that would lead to the institution of an integral nation and an integral nationality above sectional interests and above party interests, which he always despised. The interesting thing about his form of Frenchness is that everyone could have a role in it. All of the minorities which he effectively despised as foreigners, *métèques*, could actually always have a role within France. It's just their role would be lesser proportionate on who and what they are in relation to the role of the French. Ultimately, his vision was conservative. If you were more French than somebody else, you had more of a say and more of a role. If you were Catholic rather than Protestant or Jewish or something, you had more of a role in France. It was not to say the others would have no role, but they would have a severely restricted and reduced role in relation to those who would supervene over the goddess. The goddess was one of his private terms for France and for the French nation, which was always perceived as a feminine creation and identity by all of its proponents and detractors.

Charles Maurras is so French a figure that he is largely ig-
nored in the Anglophone and Anglo-Saxon world because he's
seen to have little to teach to the rival Protestant, national, and
imperial trajectories of these societies. This is arguably true.
Maurras has to be seen and judged in French terms and in
French terms alone.

Although he never succeeded in the most radical of his
aims, part of the regime that existed under Vichy can be seen as
the endorsement of many of his ideas, although the resistance
groups would pitch and the Allied invasion pulled back upon
Vichy and led to the end of the collaboration. The irony of
Maurras' tradition and career is that the sort of France he
wanted was brought about under the arms and vigilance of the
nation he hated more than any other, namely the Germans.
This is part of the irony of history, which would not be forgotten on somebody as literate and carefully-minded as Charles
Maurras.

One of the things that's most striking about Maurras is that
the *Action Française* was read intellectually right across the
spectrum. A young, homosexual Jewish author called Marcel
Proust, who was later to write one of the most famous books in
French literature, called *Remembrance of Things Past*, used to literally run every Friday down to the Camelots du Roi paramilitaries who sold *Action Française* on the streets in order to buy a
copy of *Action Française*. And when he was asked by a certain
dumbfounded bohemian of his acquaintance why he did this,
he said he did it because it was the most interesting paper in
France. And this is something which is key to an understanding of people like Maurras and the radical Right cultural tradition that they represented. They were admired by all sorts of
people who didn't share their opinions at all, and that was part
of the elixir of their power and their cultural influence. This is
why he was elected to the French Academy, the most august,
[inaudible], and antiquated of French cultural institutions.

So I think that it falls upon us, as a largely non-French people, to look back upon this traditionalist philosopher of the
French radical Right with a degree of quiet appraisal. Maurras

was a figure who could be admired as somebody who fought for his own country to the last element of his own breath. He was also somebody whose own cultural dynamics were complicated and ingenious. To give one cogent example, the Greek play *Antigone* deals with the prospect of the punishment of a woman by Creon because she wishes to honor the death sacrifice of her brother. This becomes a conflict between the state and those who would seek to supplant the state's momentary laws by laws which are regarded as matriarchal or affirmative with the chthonian or the fundamental in human life. George Steiner once commented in a book looking at the different varieties of *Antigone* that most critics of the Left have always supported her against Creon, and most socially Right-wing commentators like T. S. Eliot have always supported Creon against Antigone. And yet Maurras supported Antigone against Creon, because she wished to bury her brother for reasons which were ancestral and chthonian and came up from under the ground and were primeval and were blood-related and therefore were more important and more profound than the laws that men had put together with pieces of parchment and bits of writing on paper.

Charles Maurras: hero of France, national collaborator with excellence, we salute you over this time, we remember your contribution to the [inaudible] of a rival nationality!

Charles Maurras! Thank you very much!

MARTIN HEIDEGGER*

Martin Heidegger. Now, this talk in some respects is incredibly difficult, because I remember when the elitist Jewish academic George Steiner was asked to do the Fontana Modern Masters on Heidegger, it was because a long series of Oxbridge academics couldn't do it. They basically couldn't reduce the extraordinary complexity of, in particular this work, *Being and Time*, to one hundred pages. Because *Fontana Modern Masters*, as you know, is a students' sort of "cheat" primer, the sort of thing that people look up on the Internet now. And to reduce Heidegger to that is slightly ridiculous. But you also have to provide a sort of middling and upper-middling foregrounding for people to come into the theory anyway, otherwise they'll be at sea.

Now, what people do when they write *Times Literary Supplement*, never mind *Sunday Times*, articles about somebody like Heidegger is they basically talk about his politics; they talk about whether or not he had a mistress; they talk about his early Catholicism; they talk about wraparound and biographical matters, because the theory is amongst the most difficult metaphysical theories written in the last century.

Probably Adorno and Sartre on the ultra-Left—both of whom cross over with certain areas that Heidegger was concerned with, Sartre, biographically never mind anything else—and Heidegger are amongst the most complicated theorists that one can ever imagine. So, before we start on this talk, we have to look at what's happened to Western philosophy in the last hundred years.

Now, for those who read their philosophy at tertiary level in our universities—and tertiary education has been so degraded in many respects through egalitarian discourse that it's almost meaningless, but for those who do—they know that there ar-

---

* This lecture was delivered at the sixth English New Right meeting in London on February 18, 2006.

etwo great clusters in Western academic philosophy: so-called Anglo-American philosophy, and so-called, but essentially actual, European and Continental philosophy.

We grow up, whether we like it or not—because even the Tony Blairs of this world are actually subliminally influenced by these ideas—in an empirical, naturalist, factually-oriented, slightly anti-theoretical current which comes from our alleged and *soi-disant* Enlightenment. And we come out of an essentially an anti-theoretical and an anti-metaphysical discourse, which is why something as unbelievably *outré* as this is literally outside of British and Anglo-concentric thinking in all sorts of ways. For a long time it was said that *Being and Time* would be untranslatable, and it wasn't translated until '62. And don't forget, the book was written in the '20s. And it's translated by two academics, so it's sort of two-for-one, with Blackwells, a sort of generalized Oxbridge publisher.

Now, what is Continental philosophy trying to do, and why does Anglo-American philosophy think it's meaningless? Because these are questions that *can't be answered* and therefore shouldn't even be asked, in a Bertrand Russell and Wittgensteinian way of looking at things. Basically, Heidegger is trying, through semi-atheistic and allegedly secular discourse, to arrive at certain ultimate spiritual truths grounded in pure philosophy, and in pure thinking about thinking, even thinking about the thinking of thinking. And he is trying to prove certain cardinal things that, in many ways, gifted adolescents ask, but often as they often atrophy into adulthood and early maturity they fall away from. Most people ask, "What's life for?" "Is there a God?" "Is there ultimate purpose?" "What is death about?" "Will anything happen to me that can be acknowledged as existing before I die that impinges upon this cardinal event?" "Why are most people completely oblivious to these issues and are terrified and are often in a state of mild anxiety if they come up in general discourse?"

Now, Heidegger is trying to reach *real conclusions*, grounded philosophical conclusions, about these cardinal matters. Because he believed that Western metaphysics—and this is an incredibly arrogant statement, really—that Western metaphysics had gone wrong for two thousand five-hundred years of falsity and inauthenticity in relation to the primal nature of Being, which he believed is even a category within the notion of Being which he calls Being-in-Being.

Now, what's "Being"? The "science" of Being in abstract philosophy is called ontology, and all of his work is about ontology. Now, this slogan behind me which Troy has kindly put up is, in part, a conceit, because it says, "Martin Heidegger and Death's Ontology." Well, you can't really have an ontology of death, but you can have an ontology of life. But his whole point is to place life, as understood as concrete Being and as phenomenon, before death.

Heidegger is essentially a religious thinker, but he wants to route theoretical and theological energies through pure intellectuality. Why so? Because it is a way into intellectual understanding in the twentieth century. Most of the cardinal ideas of the twentieth century impinge upon him. And he was taught phenomenology at university by Edmund Husserl, to whom *Being and Time* is dedicated. In the sort of epigraph/frontal page he says, "Dedicated to Edmund Husserl in friendship and admiration. Black Forest 8th of April 1926."

Now, many people, sort of undergraduates, people who go on Channel 4 documentaries, would say that Martin Heidegger is an existentialist. And he influenced enormously that school, but in actual fact he is not an existentialist, hence the endless intellectual complication. He is as far removed as that, whilst being tangential to it, as one can possibly imagine. Now, he is a radical *essentialist* of the most primary and foundational form.

Most of the contemporary theory that's influenced Western university professors and other intellectuals in the last thirty years is based on a particular type of existentialism which is designed, in a way, to get rid of this sort of material even before they start thinking. The idea is that existence is all there is, and existence foregrounds essence. There is no prior essence, there are no ontological variants which could be said to be true before us. Essentially, there is—put crudely and in *Sun* editorial terms, if you can even describe Heidegger in such cultural proximities—they're saying that God is not just dead, but was always dead and was always a mistake and even the admission of his existence or partial existence was based on a question that shouldn't be asked, because it was epistemologically false even in the asking of it.

Epistemology is the science, or way, of understanding how one should think: thinking about thinking, if you like. Because in this type of thinking, before you have a thought you must, rather like a surgeon, make sure that your tools are all right in order to operate. So you have to think about the thinking you're going to initiate before you even start thinking.

Now, most Left-wing ideas are based upon the idea that we're a *tabula rasa*, that we're a sheet of paper, that society is, that you can write upon it as you want and as you will; that we're the product of economics, or that we're the product of social forces or interconnections of the two; there might be a bit of biology but it's so mediated through socioeconomic concerns that it's lost sight of. Certainly, there are no prior truths to us and our existence. Hence Sartre's famous essay which was designed to bring Leftist students, and a whole generation of them, many of whom are prominent in the media now and so on, in the Western world into a particular type of thinking. He wrote an essay called "Existentialism is a Humanism" because ultimately, in a sense, it is, although paradoxically there have been plenty of Right-wing existentialists.

They believe that existence precedes essence; essence is just an idea, is a ghost, is a spook in the machine, is that which is prior, is that which all modern theory rejected when the modern world replaced the Medieval world. And in some respects, although it's a very crude analysis, Heidegger is a supercharged modern who was a return of radically Medieval ways of looking at the world: at meaning, at purpose, at will, and at existence in existence as clarified essence. So, in a way he is trying — scribbling away at this chalet he had, made of wood in the Black Forest — to confirm the existence of God, basically. That's what he's trying to do with this enormous amount of theory.

When post-structuralism, so-called, became the cardinal intellectual discourse of our universities, pretty much in the

1980s/1990s and subsequently, those theories are based upon the idea which radicalizes even the existentialist project of the '50s and '60s. And this is that there is no essential foundation to meaning. I remember a Marxist university professor I know quite well—he teaches at some upgraded poly which is now called a university in London—Malcolm Evans, who wrote a book about Shakespeare called *Signifying Nothing*, which is a quote from *Macbeth* of course, so there's a clever interweaving of texts going on here. But he basically believes that essentialism is dangerous. Because of course, although your average Socialist Worker Party activist, and there's few of them left, would even think in these terms, it is a totally rival and totally discontinuous and totally oppositional way of thinking. They believe, they begin with man in his predicament and the only way to get out of that predicament is to change one's environment which creates the nature of that predicament.

Heidegger's view is that everything is prior, everything is prior, and death is before you. And death, in accordance with essentially his religious nature, is what life is about. In other words, life is about preparing yourself for inexistence.

Now, one of the sort of comets that goes across this constellation which could be said to be Heidegger is Jean-Paul Sartre, who did his thesis in Germany, partly during the Nazi period. Sartre, this rather sort of short-sighted ugly man, stooping around, running about, didn't seem to know what was going on in Germany at this period. Indeed, there were circles of the Left in post-war France who held it against Sartre that he actually studied in Germany during this period, influenced by these sorts of ideas.

Now, Sartre takes these ideas in another direction. So, he doesn't have a prior essence; that there are things like Beauty with a big "B," Justice with a big "J," Truth with a big "T," and so on, that exist prior to man. He believes that everything is unknown prior to specific consciousness. But you authenticate yourself and the possibility of Being by confronting nothingness and filling the emptiness with volition, in his case by choosing to be an extreme Leftist. Life is utterly meaningless. But one chooses a course for one's life and for one's discourse.

And this led him to a myopic apoliticism and moping around in German libraries in the 1930s through to Maoism, essentially, because he basically ended up in a sort of Maoist sect before he died in the 1970s. Something which, because Pol Pot of all people passed through some of those Parisian salons in the 1970s, listening to people like Kristeva and these other post-structuralist theorists, has rather doomed Sartre in post-war and after his death terms, because you can't claim existentialism as a humanism when one of your moral pupils turns out to be Pol Pot! That's been a bit difficult, you see.

But you have this extraordinary radicalism in the examples of these two men. Sartre ends up with Mao (put crudely), and Heidegger ends up with Hitler. Because both of them, if you like, begin thinking cardinally about the values of our civilization which, when you think about it logically, would lead them to some of the most radical conclusions, socially, politically, and ideologically, which are possible.

Because this type of intellectuality—and I'm going to read certain sections of it because there is a pretension always to talking about people like Heidegger without dealing with what we'll call the hard core; you've actually got to look at the material which is written in a sedentary way, but is written, in a sense, in accordance with the notion of intellectual fury. It's a belief that all of life and all of meaning can be revealed through mental processes, which I don't believe is true, but it's a heroic attempt to do this.

And this sort of language is virtually a system of thinking which has more relationship with artistic ways of describing things, actually. Because Heidegger's theory is something that you have to experience. Here is a man dwelling upon ultimate questions of whether there is an essence in an essence, of what it means to be you, or this table, or anything that phenomenologically exists. Or, are there realms above us or beneath us or around us? And, how can you answer a moral question with an affirmative statement?

Wittgenstein's point in *Tractatus* and after is that ultimately you can't answer a morally affirmative statement, because to do so is meaningless outside language, and language is all that exists, and language is given even only a partial meaning through context. There's a famous and funny story of Wittgenstein where he's ferociously berating an American visiting professor at Cambridge and he says, "You can't make affirmative moral statements," and he's waving a poker in his face. And the university professor replies, "Here's an affirmative moral statement: 'Don't wave pokers in the faces of visiting professors.'" And Wittgenstein hurls the poker into the fire and storms out of the room in a rant.

But these attempts, abstract and very radical though they are, always, like Icarus in a sense, go up and then come down again. Because, mark my words, every politician and every pundit, no matter how low-level, no matter how two hundred times beneath this sort of discourse they are, is actually replicating ideas that have come from somewhere and are going somewhere. The reason why—you know, you walk around London today—the world is as it is, is ideological in the broadest of senses. Because a man who has any sort of belief becomes the equivalent of fifty men in action. And Heidegger was a man whose action was theory in this purely Germanic way.

I met a German intellectual once and he said, "Ah, you're an intellectual," and he sits down, and he looks right into your eyes, and you begin the theory. This is a totally un-British sort of way of behaving because there's no concept of irony in a way, but this idea that you achieve truth through almost a violence of intellectuality, which in a way Heidegger evinces.

Now, let's read something from *Being and Time*. Now, *Being and Time* is divided into two books, essentially. The first one is "An Explanation of the Question of the Meaning of Being; The Necessity, Structure, and Priority of the Question of Being." This is whether we can even talk about the nature of talking about the book. We have, "The Necessity for Explicitly Restating the Question of Being," we have "The Formal Structure of the Question of Being," we have "The Ontological Priority of the Question of Being," and we have "The Ontical Priority of the Question of Being." That takes him thirty-two pages before he's even started. You've got to clear away all the sort of refuse in your garden before you start, basically.

Part One is "The Interpretation of Dasein in Terms of Temporality," that means the interpretations of Being in terms of time, and "The Explication of Time as the Transcendental Horizon for the Question of Being." Then there's another section about "Being-in-the-world in General as the Basic State of Dasein." Then there's a section on "The Worldhood of the World," by which he means, "Is the world as we appear?" Can we prove that you are actually there? Because it's actually very difficult from first principles to prove common sense: that I'm speaking to you, that I'm not speaking to myself, that it's a vision, that I'm talking about things that are endlessly solipsistic, in pure mental processes without being empirical, because this type of theory believes that empiricism distorts because you go down to matter, and so you must keep it totally at a theoretical level. It's actually quite difficult to prove the idea that everything isn't an idea, and that even addressing you in this way is an idea, and so on.

"Being-in-the-World as Being-with and Being-one's-Self, the 'They'." This is the idea that one approaches the possibility of semi-existence in another, theoretically, before one gets there. Then we have "Being-in as Such." Intellectual Germans love these little "as suches" and so on. "Care as the Being of Dasein," now this is the self-reflexiveness of the possibility of Being-in-Being. What does he mean by "Being-in-Being"? He really means the presence of God in life. Really, deep down, in my view, he never left the Jesuits who trained him intellectually, and his thesis was on Duns Scotus; the idea that everything is, essentially, foregrounded before one gets there, theoretically.

Here's the second book, Division Two. "Dasein and Temporality; Dasein's Possibility of Being-a-Whole and Being-Towards-Death," which is the real point, to place man in full understanding of it before death.

Now, there's always with this sort of theory, possibly a sort of alienation effect. But the way to look at it is there are few moments of profundity in most individual's lives, but one of them is that period when one is probably pretty conscious that one is waiting for death. And it's going to happen to all of us, you and me, and in some ways the way to overcome the sort of innate philistinism that exists about this pure, pure theory is to put yourself in that position. Because Heidegger's work is a man in early life in full consciousness of radical mental gifts, thinking about what it means to die before you get there, and not responding at the level of emotion. Although I believe personally that all theory is physically based and comes out of the emotions as part of one's physicality, but let's not intrude my ideas too much.

Another section is "Dasein's Attestation of an Authentic Potentiality-for-Being, and Resoluteness." Another section is "Dasein's Authentic Potentiality-for-Being-a-Whole, and Temporality as the Ontological Meaning of Care." Then there's a section on "Temporality and Everydayness." By this time we've got up to page 421, by the way. Then there's a section on "Temporality and Historicality," and then there's a section on "Temporality and Within-Time-ness as the Source of the Ordinary Conception of Time." Then there's some dealings with other theorists who are also brushed away at the end, Hegel in particular.

The last section of all, which is Section 83, around pages 436 to 486, is "The existential-temporal analysis of Dasein, and the question of fundamental ontology as to the meaning of Being in general." This is the moment when he wants to place man before death, self-aware of the nature of authentic existence.

As a critique of all this sort of material Adorno—in some respects his chief ideological nemesis on the other side—wrote a book called *The Jargon of Authenticity*, which is an attack upon this type of thinking. Adorno is one of the key thinkers in what's called Western Marxism and the Frankfurt School.

Now, here is a section on death, because it's all essentially about death. "Underlying this biological-ontical exploration of death"—that just means the biological exploration of death—"is a problematic that is ontological." That concerns the science of Being.

We still have to ask how the ontological essence of death is defined in terms of that of life. In a certain

way, this has always been decided already in the ontical investigation of death. Such investigations operate
with preliminary conceptions of life and death, which
have been more or less clarified.

That's in the last 290 pages, which I'll forebear from reading
out. "These preliminary conceptions need to be sketched out by
the ontology of Dasein." Which is Being-in-Being.

Within the ontology of Dasein, which is *superordinate*
to an ontology of life, the existential analysis of death
is, in turn, *subordinate* to a characterization of Dasein's
basic state. The ending of that which lives we have
called 'perishing.' Dasein too 'has' its death, of the
kind appropriate to anything that lives.

And basically he's asking here, does what traditionalist orders
have called the soul survive death?

And it has it, not in ontical isolation, but as codeter-
mined by its primordial kind of Being. In so far as this
is the case, Dasein too can end without authentically
dying, though on the other hand, *qua* Dasein, it does
not simply perish. We designate this intermediate
phenomenon as its *'demise'*.

Then there's a large footnote which I'll forebear from going into because it's printed in point 6, I think. "Let the term *'dying'*
stand for that *way of Being* in which Dasein *is towards* its death."
Auxiliary footnote. "Accordingly we must say that Dasein never perishes. Dasein, however, can demise only as long as it is
dying." So, he's talking about the death of the concept of the
soul which is self-aware of the possibility of that moment,
okay? "Medical and biological investigation into 'demising' can
obtain results which may even become significant ontologically
if the basic orientation for an existential interpretation of death
has been made secure." Ah ha! "Or must sickness and death in
general—even from a medical point of view"—notice: "medical

point of view"; physical stuff which we keep out of sight—"be primarily conceived as existential phenomena?"

The first thing that strikes you about this is his attitude towards death. You walk round a death ward in a hospital—you know they're all about to give out—most people's response is physical and emotional, the one and the other. He regards that as bourgeois deviation; even as filth. Always keep your theory before you because that's how you apprise the nature of that which is real as against that which is mere appearance, and that which is governed by dread.

In the 1960s the counter-culture, that had many tendencies which ultimately tended overwhelmingly to the Left regardless of this, had the notion that life was not as it should be or could be. That there needed to be a spiritual dimension to human beings that had been lost sight of, given the collapse of the Christian religion. And I take it as unarguable that in our civilization in the last hundred years, in accordance with what it once was, in the West largely, with the odd exception, individual and group, the Christian religion has collapsed. And it's collapsed amongst the most advanced thinkers of our civilization and racial or ethnic group from early in the nineteenth century. Or at least they were aware of the possibility of its mass collapse long before it became a sociological phenomenon. This is why this theory, which ultimately has had much more impact in theology than it has in philosophy, has been put in this particular way.

Now, this book has over 460 pages. And when the Renaissance occurred in our thinking, one of the great criticisms of the philosophical schools that preceded it, of which Duns Scotus was an accredited master, was that they were dealing with things that could never be proved at this level of reality, even theoretically. And the slogan that's used is that they were debating the number of angels that could dance on the head of a pin. And it was all utterly pointless, and we had to get away from all of that.

Now, Heidegger wants to go back there, up to a point, but in actual fact he wants to go even further back. He wants to go back to the pre-Socratics, he wants to go back to the Sophists, he wants to go back to the original and primary Greek thinkers that begin the process two-and-a-half thousand years ago, which is why Nietzsche obsessed him. Because, if you like, Nietzsche stands halfway between this radical essentialist/quasi-religious thinking, that there is before you nothing but God, and God in all and God for all, and you're part of him. Which, if you sacralize this language, begins to make sense of what Being is, what Being-in-Being is, what Being-in-Being before all Being is, and so on. It's, if you like, a re-rooted theological language use. There's that position. And prior traditionalists who have Right-wing views largely accord philosophically and psychologically with this area.

Nietzsche, who's a figure who obsessed Heidegger of course, and who has this enormous theoretical explosion at the end of the nineteenth century, just preceding the emergence of people like Husserl, Jaspers, and Heidegger, in early twentieth century Germanic thinking at a high philosophical level. Don't forget, Anglo-American philosophy almost denies the possibility of metaphysics. Bertrand Russell would say, if he were sat at the back, which is a bit difficult considering he's been a corpse for about thirty years, but he would say, "It's all meaningless. It's an interesting talk, but it's about things that can't be proved at any level and is therefore pointless. Because your view is as good as his, as good as so-and-so's. The only difference is people can put it better, or worse. But there can be no grounded truth that I can grasp and put social practice and purpose to."

Now, Nietzsche stands halfway between the Left existentialist view, that there's nothing prior, that, put very simply, we make it up as we go along.

Baudrillard, a French intellectual, wrote a book in the 1990s saying that the first Gulf War was just a computer game; it didn't happen. Didn't happen, it was just a discourse. All those cluster bombs and stealth bombs and so on, it was just a fantasy in a televisual age: one man's discourse, you see?

In an age of extreme relativism, which is the almost opposite of this absolutist theory, totalitarian theory, which is actually, mentally what it is, we see the division between what exists now and the reasons for some of the very controversial, certainly in the mainstream, political choices that Heidegger made in the middle of his life in Germany in the '30s.

Now, Nietzsche's position is that there is a prior, there is an essence, but Nietzsche is a partial to semi-absolute existential thinker. Because Nietzsche's contribution to modernity and to modern intellectual thinking is there may be things which are prior, but we don't know what they are, and we have to test them through struggle, through life, through will and purposiveness, and various levels of what he called Will to Power, which he believed was the basis of all lived existence.

So, Nietzsche says God is dead partly to say he's a militant atheist, but partly to say that the idea of God in the minds of men has died, which means that theoretically it may not have completely died but is in a point of collapse. Because the point is to test and to rearrange, and you put up a view and I will attack it because life is struggle. And in that struggle comes out the possibility of meaning. Nietzsche would say, "There is a truth, but I don't know it yet. Go and buy me another drink." There is a degree to which ontological circumstances cannot be completely proved but are not rendered prior meaningless, which is why Nietzsche approaches nihilism, the belief that there is no purpose and no values and no constraints and no morals that aren't purely human, and that there is nothing outside. Which, of course, makes it very difficult to run any sort of a civilization, because there are no lines.

And Nietzsche stands halfway between what you might call this existential Leftist praxis and Heidegger. Nietzsche's become extremely fashionable on the Left in the last thirty years, and there's lots of postmodernist books by people like Deleuze and Guattari, and these sorts of people, who love the element of Nietzsche that tears down—"I come as a destroyer!"—because in order to create you've got to destroy first, you've got to level off a bit. There's ruins around you, so you give them a bit of a push.

All of Nietzsche's thinking before *Zarathustra*, when he begins to vouchsafe his own view, if you like, is largely a tearing down: a tearing down of the normative nature of ethics in *The*

Genealogy of Morals; tearing down of the idea of truth itself; an erection of science in works like *The Dawn* or *The Joyful Wisdom/The Gay Science*; and then a tearing down of the idea of science; a playing up of certain Darwinian and evolutionary ideas which Nietzsche's actually quite suspicious of because he doesn't think that life and circumstances are linear at all, he believes they're circular, and everything that was comes back again. He thinks that Darwinists are cretinous materialists and shallow optimists. Look at people around you. Are they progressing and moving upwards, or are they just dullards led by a few people at the top who manipulate them?

Now, Heidegger made a radical, possibly the most radical, choice philosophically and politically in the century that's just passed. Admittedly, he was living in Germany at a time when, if the Left-liberal consensus would have it, the most controversial regime in the twentieth century came to power. Now, if you were in other races or in other societies you would actually refute that, you'd say that Stalin's or Lenin's or Mao's or various other regimes were more important. You could argue that the most important regime in the twentieth century is the American one. But put all that on another table for today.

Heidegger decided in 1933 to join the Nazi Party, to join the National Socialist German Workers' Party and gave lectures for a year in his university in full Nazi uniform[1] and was involved with all of the other Party *Gauleiters* and other figures in his area to the shock and horror and consternation of much of the academic elite that he was associated with. And don't forget that Heidegger did this for purely speculative and theoretical reasons. Heidegger had no concern with doctrines of race, no concerns with doctrines of conspiracy, no concerns with politics at all. Politics was irrelevant in relation to placing man before death, which is what life was about. And what he loved about this movement was that he thought it was a primordial movement that was bringing back, almost in an occultistic way, the partiality towards death, and in some ways it was bringing

---

[1] Heidegger was not a member of the SA or SS. Therefore, he did not have a "Nazi uniform." —Ed.

back the ancient world with modern technology. That's why he
reached out to it.

Now, he regarded democracy, just like middle-brow secular
humanism, as a deviation. Because in a sense his nature is so
primordially prior and religious that he considers almost all
normal life to be irrelevant: family, having a good time, pleasure, pleasure as a principle for life, which in liberal theory is
cardinal. The American Constitution talks about liberty, talks
about property, talks about happiness. Heidegger doesn't think
the purpose of life is happiness; the purpose of life is *death* and
facing ontology. But he doesn't put it in the vocabulary that
you must fall before the one who is on the cross and who
bleeds for us because, in a sense, Heidegger just increasingly
sees those as forms of metaphysics for metaphysics, stuff that
needs to be put out of the way so one can concentrate on the
cardinal things of life, death, spirituality, and the possible existence of God.

"God," as he told Paul Celan when they met in '67, "has always been with me." Celan is interesting, of course, a Jewish
poet who wrote in German for which he was condemned by
his own group and converted to Catholicism because of
Heidegger's influence. And that was not a sectarian influence,
because Heidegger was totally uninterested in what sect people
were in, and so on. These were all forms that have no importance.

And in some ways there's a great paradox, because
Heidegger's thinking is so purely, transcendently extreme that
he's one of the few figures where the pagan/Christian split in
our civility doesn't really mean anything to him. This is one of
the things that interests me very much about him. With this
Right-wing group, for example, a few Christians turned up early, they went, and it's largely pagan in orientation. In the New
Right in Europe, and so on, you have this very great split between the two. Heidegger's almost totally unconcerned with
those things because the forms that people worship Being-in-
Being through are incidental to placing man before ontological
prerequisites.

His view is that you base life and society upon the profound thinking that will impinge upon a man of full consciousness, not physically debilitated, before his moment of death. And that's why he joined the Nazi Party. That's why virtually no one could understand why he'd joined it, because he was totally sort of unorthodox in ideological terms because he had very little interest in that.

After a year he sort of realized that, one, probably at a crude level they didn't understand what he was on about; two, that he was having to make political decisions in the university, the library, its use and so on that he didn't agree with. And he fell away. He left the Party then[2] and continued to teach in the University until 1945. In '45 he was proscribed by the de-Nazification tribunals that were set up in the Western Allied zones. Now, he was forbidden from teaching in post-war Germany even though all sorts of people had him as a guest lecturer, so they used to get around it that way. And you have this strange situation where he became a sort of moral and spiritual leper in post-war Germany, and yet he was extremely respected. So Dr. Heidegger, Professor Heidegger, was everywhere, but at the same time he didn't even have a university post.

And there's all sorts of interesting things because Husserl taught him, and because Husserl was a Jew he was banned from the University library, but after the war Heidegger was banned from the library. And Jaspers wrote to educational authorities in Germany saying he shouldn't be given a post. So you have all of this as well.

There was a play a couple of weeks ago on the BBC by John Banville, an Irish writer, about Heidegger that was very interesting. And it's a dramatization, because all dramatists are interested in dialectic. They're interested in two minds if it's a theoretical play of any sort, two minds coming together that disagree, and the tension and the charge and the flow of energy that occurs between those two minds, and whether you can make a narrative out of it that can be listened to from beginning to end. And it's this talk in his hut in the Black Forest.

---

[2] Heidegger resigned from the Rectorate but did not resign from the Party. He remained a member until the end in 1945. —Ed.

Because, very interestingly, there is almost inevitably a monastic element to Heidegger. Heidegger is into the woods in primal inner Germany. To sit there in the middle of this forest and dwell upon death. And write a book of 450 pages of — probably to certain Anglo-Saxon minds — sheer intellectual torture, virtually, in order to get *nearer to the truth* that is the truth that is the truth, that will not set you free but release you to die with some dignity. Because that's the only truth that matters. And there's a sort of divine element to it in a way because it's so near to the inexpressible.

Artistically, of course in a blowback sense, it's had an enormous influence on novelists in Germany like Hermann Broch and these sorts of things, he wrote *The Death of Virgil*, and he wrote a book called *The Sleepwalkers*, and so on. And this extraordinary capacity for intellectual abstraction that many German writers have, they begin with a relatively straightforward narrative and suddenly lurch off into ultimate speculative questions, very much influenced by this type of theory.

But I don't think people who are illiberal can understand the shock in liberal intellectual elitist circles of a man like Heidegger joining the Nazi Party. It is actually slightly emotionally difficult to describe it. From a sort of view of BBC culture it is *the worst thing*, and not just the worst thing but beyond the worst, that one could do. This man of supreme intellectual gifts dwelling alone in his Shavian hut in the woods dwelling on the ontology of death in life in death in life in death in life — do you see what I mean? — joins, what they considered to be, a barbarous wrecking crew. And they're appalled, they're utterly morally appalled. And since the War, people have not really known what to do with Heidegger at all.

And because, in a sense, his theory is an attempt to bring back a different version of the West's civilization, most people who were on the side politically that he associated with, albeit for a period, didn't know how to make use of him either, in a strange sort of way. That's why he's this sort of illisible figure. It's noticeable in Tomislav Sunić's book on the New Right, for instance. Heidegger in a way can't be integrated. It's a sort of cigarette on the paper that burns through to the other side. He really is in a zone on his own.

And what's he trying to do? He's trying to see whether human beings can live authentically. There's a moment in Nietzsche's letters early on in his theoretical course/development/ prognosis after the first text, *Birth of Tragedy*, when he describes seeing a goatherd killing a goat on a hill—I think it's in Italy— and it's what James Joyce would call an epiphany. It's a moment of total, in his terms, authentication and realization. It's a poetic moment. It's what certain natures call a perfect moment. A moment that certain consciousnesses will look at before they die as the one moment that was perfect: the sky, and the goat, and the man, and the soil, and the Sun. And, essentially, it's a religious moment; it's a sort of cosmotheist moment, in a way.

And Heidegger's point is to get people to experience such moments, which is why he writes this enormous theory to try and intellectually prepare people for the possibility of having such moments. Which is why, of course, when people try and stimulate themselves to have such moments—they chant; they sing; they starve themselves; they go without; they live ascetically; they do things to alter consciousness. In a sense he just deals with pure consciousness because he doesn't, almost, relate to the physical level at all.

But it is an attempt to go back to what many Western and Indo-European theorists have believed was cardinal at the beginning of Greek culture. It's Nietzsche's view and it's other people's view that the Greek tragedians—the great three, Aeschylus, Sophocles, and Euripides—that there is a "decadence." That in a sense, Aeschylus is the most hieratic, the most removed from everyday, the most transcendental, the most *ur*-ascending.

Sophocles is not a humanist by any means—there's the matter of the Theban plays, of course—but it's a step down from that sense of mystery, that sense of sort of sheer awe. We now live in a society without any sense of the sacred at all, as de Benoist has pointed out. It's virtually void.

And a level down in this trajectory involving the Greek tragic writers is Euripides. He's hardly writing soap opera, but where the gods and the goddesses are seen almost, if not level with human beings, then as superhumans who are just a couple of levels up. But they relate to each other, they fight with each other, they make love to each other, and all this sort of thing, in a way which is recognizably humanesque.

And, in a way, you could metaphoracize it, because with theory like this that's all you really can do, certainly in a talk of this nature. Those prior moments when Aeschylus looks at the divine—because don't forget, Western theatre begins with religious ritual and gradually separates itself out—it begins with a monologue, and then Aeschylus has the idea this is going on a bit too long, so we'll split it and we'll have a duologue, and the two consciousnesses talk to each other. And in that you have the tension with which you can sustain drama in our culture, in any culture.

Now, in this theatricalization of this meeting in the hut in the woods where he wrote *Being and Time* and where he wrote other books on Greek tragedy and on Nietzsche, Celan and Heidegger have this talk. And this is Banville dreaming. But this type of theory is actually quite close to forms of artistic creation; forms of higher, non-entertainment-based spiritual creation in art forms. And Celan says, "Why did you join the Nazi Party?" And Heidegger replies, "Because they were the one movement of the twentieth century that, in my terms, had a tragic view of life. That had a view of life which is actually the motif and the inner essence—*Dasein*—of the Greek tragedians taken up to date two and a half thousand years later." And I think that's essentially a truthful statement.

He gave an interview to the *Spiegel* magazine after his death, in the sense that it was recorded before his death but could only be published as part of his will and settlement after his demise. I think it was published about three, four weeks after he died. And they ask him, because it was a very adversarial interview while he was alive, post-dated as I say, about why he'd joined, why he did this, why he did that, and so on. And in actual fact there's lots of evasion and attempts at exculpation and bringing in all the usual things, and even though political correctness wasn't a buzzword then, he's in some ways playing games. He's like a politician on the defensive.

But in actual fact, as often with art in my view, you've got to cut to the truth suddenly through all sorts of layers, even if the person never said it, it can actually illuminate because it crystallizes in a form the value of something. And when he says to Celan, with no one there, in this fantasy—because Celan didn't go and see him in that hut for nothing, just so he could put his name in Heidegger's signature book, "I've been up to the professor's lodge"—people at this sort of level don't do those sorts of things. He wanted to know why, as George Steiner said, one of, if not the most, advanced theoretical minds of the Western civilization in the twentieth century adopted this particular course.

And he did it because he believed that you cannot have a society where death has no meaning, because life has no meaning. And you cannot have a society which bases itself upon the absence of the religious urge, however you define that urge and whatever system you use. Because if you do the reverse, you will end up with a society which has two values beyond subsistence. And that could be seen in the title of a grubby play produced in London a couple of years ago called *Shopping and Fornication*. But that is all that life is, if you do not have spiritual levels based upon that.

People will always be completely divided about the forms and the language that they use to talk about cardinal matters. But in a way, in a quite moving way really, Heidegger is attempting to get people to face in early modernity what it means to have a civilization and, not to be human, but to live with profound and real meaning. And there's no doubt that this theoretical postulation and this extreme abstraction is quite alien to elements of the Western civilization, certainly our own quadrant of it during the last couple of hundred years. But it is an attempt, not to aestheticize life, but to place life, ultimately, at the service of God, even and most especially for people who either don't believe in him or can only approach such numinence through endless tiers of theory.

Thank you very much!

SAVITRI DEVI*

Savitri Devi was born in September of 1905 and died aged 77 in 1982. Now Savitri Devi is extraordinarily radical and is amongst one of the most *extreme* and militant individuals that I've ever discussed. I've had talks about Julius Evola, and I've had talks about Friedrich Nietzsche in the past. I've had talks about metapolitical and cultural figures who overlap with the radical Right. Probably you couldn't really begin to imagine anyone *more* militant than her, so I think it's best to step back from the immediate biography and the welter of detail and look at the thing philosophically.

She was half-English, which is often rarely thought or mentioned on the Internet and elsewhere, and she died here *en route* to a provocative meeting, we'll say, in the United States. One of the things that's most abiding about her, and that interests me a great degree, is the degree of her intelligence. This is one of the most extraordinary things. Extremism and militancy in contemporary liberal societies are often associated in the mass mind with stupidity, or ignorance, or bigotry, and this sort of thing. And this woman could speak eight languages, read eight languages. She had two Master's degrees, one in chemistry and one in philosophy, and she had a PhD in mathematics,[1] which, given that her future career, if you like on the political margin, so to speak, mathematics is quite interesting, but I think also cardinal for the type of radicalism/extremism she would develop later in her life and ideological course.

Now, in many forms of mathematics, of course, you're looking for X; you're looking for what the sort of alternative middle-rank thinker Colin Wilson called Faculty X. You've got an equation, and you have to find X and maybe balance a particu-

---

* This lecture was delivered to the twenty-ninth English New Right meeting in London on October 23, 2010. The transcript was made by R. F.
[1] Savitri's PhD was in philosophy, but her dissertation was on the philosophy of mathematics. —Ed.

lar equation, a particular quantity on either side of the equals sign. And in a sense, mathematical truth is pushing prognosticated truths to the absolute limit of their efficacy. It's the truth within the truth, beyond the truth, and at the edge of a particular dispensation of thinking.

Her idea, which may or may not have been drawn from her mathematical studies when she was a young student at the University of Lyons, was the idea that if you take various forms of equation and you make a graphic form, the idea is that the line which penetrates the circle furthest away from the arc of a circle is the point of truth, is where X is, in one way of looking at it. And the idea that the truth lies at the most extreme part of the axis, the idea that rather than the safe middle, or the comfortable middle ground, truth is radical extremity, is something that she would essentially live through for most of her life.

Her father was French but of largely Italian descent and Greek descent, and she was strongly influenced by Greek thinking and supported Greek nationalist positions up until around the Great War, when she first became reasonably politically conscious. She then moved on from that afterwards. It's noticeable that because of her sort of mixed European ancestry—a bit Greek, bit French, bit Italian, half-English—she considered herself to essentially be European. And that judgment for, rather than linked, to any particular nationality or nation-state, and that judgment formed early on.

Now, her first political and ideological positions were a return to Greece, an exemplification of the Aryan culture and Indo-European culture of the ancient Greeks, a belief that the Greeks had much to tell to modern civilization. Notice this was way before any movements or regimes formed by those movements had been formed in the twentieth century. The return to Greece, the recognition of the importance of Greek thought and open-ended identity, the culture of beauty of the body, the culture of serenity, the culture of proportion and form, Classicism. Very, very important for her. And the belief that a pagan society should be a living identity, should actually be alive rather than tiny little groups, fringe little tendencies of opinion and identity in the Western world.

She made some radical decisions after her education basically came to an end, and one of them was to go to India, where she became a Hindu and was widely associated with the Hindu nationalist movement in India and fascistic forms of the Hindu nationalist movement in the 1930s and '40s. Now the figure of the white Hindu has certain resonances in Indian life, which are quite paradoxical and often militant and extreme.

What Western societies do in relation to Second and Third and Fourth World countries about which they know nothing — whilst professing to love and adore them to the end of time — is to take leaders who can be adopted and successfully acclimatized to the norms of a particular Western establishment. Like America's chosen leader of conscience who now has a day named after him as a public holiday in the United States, is Martin Luther King. But other leaders, like Stokely Carmichael and Malcolm X and Elijah Muhammad and these sorts of people are largely forgotten and deliberately moved to the side so that all of the light can fall upon "Dr." King.

Similarly, in South Africa, Nelson Mandela has gone through a secular canonization, whereas the Pan Africanist Congress and militant Communist cadres within the South African ANC — militant links with terrorist organizations in the paramilitary and military wing of the ANC, Spirit the Nation — are all elided and removed.

Hindu nationalist politics is largely seen for Westerners today through the retrospective prism of Gandhi: Gandhi's nonviolence, Gandhi's pacifism, and Gandhi's desire to have the British leave India, as indeed occurred in 1947 when the Raj came to an end and when the flag was hauled down by Mountbatten. But *she* looks for harder and more resonant individuals within Hindu nationalism.

There's always been a Hindu fascism of course, namely the RSS. And the BJP, which certain Indians within Britain secretly, behind their hands, call the BNP of India, is a populist and democratic split from the RSS. It is also important to point out that all of these organizations were involved in enormous and sub-genocidal communitarian violence at the end of the 1940s, when the Raj came to an end.

Her early publications were in favor of Hindu unity, and essentially a mainstream Hindu nationalist position. She later moved to essays discussing the roles of non-Hindus in India, which is always complicated in relation to a Hindu national consciousness. She knew virtually every leader of what would become post-war India. She also knew very well those Indian leaders who were pro-Axis and pro-German, of which there was a wide number.

Bose, for example, and his paramilitary army, the Indian National Army, is almost not mentioned at all in British historiography of the Indian subcontinent of that time, partly because he led a militant, subcontinental IRA against British rule and allied himself with Nazi Germany and with Imperial Japan against our interests. Very interestingly, in the last couple of years, documents have come to light where Bose was sentenced to death by the British cabinet, to be killed on sight by the Special Operations Executive or the SOE, if ever caught in British gunsights because he worried us, because he was aligned with core British statal enemies, the alleged Arab decision for Britain in 1939–1940.

The Hindu phase for Savitri Devi/Maximiani Portas, is her belief that there should be a living paganism rather than a dead one, and her belief in certain primal Hindu beliefs which are mainstream, completely mainstream in Hindu society and in the Asian subcontinent: the belief that Hinduism is a partly racial religion, the belief that whites or partly-whites formed it; the belief — semi-mythological, to mythological, to semi-actual — to be believed in the minds of tens and tens of millions, that certain tribes came down from the Caucasus a certain number of years, thousands of years ago, millennia ago, placed a caste religion within India whereby you can't breed with people outside the caste that you're in. This was later to completely break down and become endlessly confused. But these elements and these tendencies — the use of the fire wheel, the worship of the Sun, the belief in polytheism of the most militant sort, which has one flame possibly behind it, a sort of secret, semi-monotheism within a religion that appears to be anything but that.

Her position in Hinduism is slightly complicated and in some ways she is a perennialist, like Evola, who called himself a Catholic pagan. If you want a religion as the basis of your political attitudes; if you want something that you consider to be absolute, or a system of belief; not Tony Blair saying, "These are my views, what are yours?" Not the views of contemporary politicians. If you want something that is absolute and as she conceives it, things that people will live and die for, and fight for, in real historical time, you have to have things that are *above* and *beyond* man. You have to have things of metaphysical veracity and objectivism. In where theology merges in with philosophy, there's this idea of metaphysical objectivism: truths that are believed to be outside man and are taken as absolutes.

The contemporary mind finds a lot of this way of proceeding and looking at things extraordinarily difficult, not just because of the possible political and ideological and social consequences that can emerge from it, but also because of the mindset that it involves. When Evola talked about being a Catholic pagan, he basically meant that if you look into my face, you see ancient Rome. The name of his religion is *Roman* Catholicism, and to him he sees Antiquity and the pagan world peering straight out of Christianity. Many people believe of course that Protestantism and the Protestant Reformation is the more Judaic form of Christianity within Christianity. Whereas Catholicism does retain in its architecture, in its aesthetics, in the Renaissance, certain elements of the restitution of the ancient world, which is really what people like her wanted.

The decision to become a Hindu is very, very radical, and very absolutist, and at one level cuts you off from most white people, including quite white politically militant people elsewhere in the world. But one of the things that's rather interesting about her radicalism is the divorce between how the far Right is perceived by much of the rest of the contemporary world and many of the people who've actually been leading individuals within it.

There is the view that the radical Right exists only *against*—against other groups—against groups that it blames modernity and liberal egalitarian leveling for. Against ethnic, racial, sexual, and other minorities and so on. Her view, of course, is pretty much the other way round, in that these radical tendencies of opinion exist *for* things, and by virtue of being *for* things very radically, you will inevitably disprivilege and move slightly to the side that which you don't really approve of. So there's a degree to which her desire for an *absolute* culture that was non-Christian, and that was still a living culture that hundreds of millions adhered to, shows the depth of her extremity and the depth of her radicalism.

There's also a degree to which she was very uninterested in Mussolini's Italy, or Franco's Spain, or Salazar's Portugal, or movements elsewhere. There was a certain comment, and there was a certain interest, but it's noticeable that when she later came to adopt the view that German National Socialism was the recrudescence of extreme paganism in the Western world for man then and today and tomorrow, she came to that view unerringly because her viewpoint always goes for the most extreme and the most militant option. In some ways because of her motivation is in many respects primarily religious, she's opposed to all forms of political temporizing.

What's called populism[2] is the desire that you meet people halfway with the predilections that they already have. Radical Right parties in Europe and elsewhere go to the population after sixty years of liberal beliefs when virtually everyone has some sort of liberal belief system, no matter how marginal, even if it's only two percent of their beliefs. Populism goes to them as a political gesture and tries to hook the individual or group concerned, and bring them in to a more Rightist, traditional, perennial, authoritarian, semi-democratic, patriotic nexus, and so forth.

Her view is very much *anti-political* in one sense. She believes in going for the most extreme and the most radical option in all areas. If she wants to be a pagan, she becomes a Hindu; if she wants to be a pagan in political modernity, she be-

---

[2] Bowden is using "populism" to mean something like what is called in nationalist circles "mainstreaming." —Ed.

comes a National Socialist; if she's a National Socialist, she supports the SS, as the most militant part of National Socialism. Always with her the most extreme, the most radical option, but not as emotional fervor — although there is a certain fervid quality to her prose that can't be denied — but almost with a degree of mathematical logic and forethought whereby the most radical position leads logically and inescapably to all other positions.

Now, why did she reject Christianity in such a militant way? Essentially because it doesn't accord with her nature and essentially because of her view of both ethics and natural process. When the New Right was formed, quite a few Christian people came along early, and we had an Orthodox minister or even a bishop, I think, in the first meeting. Yet radical Right groups that have had a cultural struggle element such as this one nearly always have a split, where they're either designated as pagan, and the Christians leave; or Christian, and the pagans leave. Or there's an uneasy sort of co-relation between the two of them.

Now she believed in a total return to that which was before Christianity. She believes that essentially, Christianity is not just a Jewish religion but a universalist faith, and she's quite hostile to Islam as well, although later she would know certain individuals who settled in Nasser's Egypt and who converted to Islam and were ex-members of the Freikorps and ex-members of the NSDAP both in the '30s and '40s, and going back to the Freikorps in the early 1920s and late second decade of the last century. For those who are not aware, the Freikorps were of course those paramilitary organizations formed in June in defeat to prevent Bolshevik revolution spreading across the German heartline, to engage in fighting in the Baltic, and also just to impose order in a totally chaotic, defeated, hungry, and demoralized nation that had lost the first World War in human history, certainly within modernity.

So Savitri Devi's radicalism and the religious urge which exists behind it is evident from the very beginning. Many believe that she is attempting to create a religion out of Nazism, and indeed, many spokesmen on the radical Right, like Revilo P.

Oliver, said that after the war. "I do believe that a Hitler cult is being created," Revilo once said, "by a knowledgeable woman of Greek ancestry." And there is a degree to which you can see part of the logic of her progression in that way.

She produced a whole series of books after she came back to Europe after the German defeat in 1945. Before she left, and in the mid- to late-'30s, she married an Indian Brahmin called Mukherji. And the marriage is believed to be celibate because he was a yogic individual who believed, as ascetics do and as puritans believed in our national revolution in the 1600s, that if you deny excess or sensuality in one area, you redirect that power into another area.

Also Indian groups published most of her pro-Axis material after the war, when virtually nobody on Earth would have published that sort of material, apart from tiny little NS networks in the United States and maybe in South Africa. Virtually no one else would have published this material. She moves from the Hindu nationalist position of the late 1930s to adopt, after a break, a strident pro-Nationalist Socialist position.

She goes to Germany immediately after the Second [World] War in the mid- to late-'40s, when Germany is in total chaos. Germany has been occupied. The eastern zone, which she couldn't particularly visit because nobody from western origination could, was under Ulbricht's control.

The statistics vary, as all of these exterminationist *cum* revisionist ones do. The German parliament has declared that two million Germans died as a result of the devastation after 1945. Hundreds of thousands of German women were raped by Soviet troops in the eastern zone as a direct order which came from above. Mass armies rarely engage in rape unless it's ordered from above, or unless the restrictions upon it are ameliorated and withdrawn by an officer caste that gives approval to it. There will always be men who don't engage in those sorts of activities of course, in any army, but if it is permitted from above, the adoption that women are part of the booty of war will take hold, particularly in a group that desires radical vengeance.

The interesting thing is that in order to stop the mass raping, which was demanded by pleas of East German Communists so that they could form a state in the devastated eastern zone of Germany that was occupied by the Red Army, large numbers of men had to be shot because they had become addicted to rape, essentially, and the commissars needed to re-impose order.

This doesn't also account for the hundreds and hundreds of thousands who went through de-Nazification process, at the top of the hill and at the bottom of the hill. Lower ranking people—orderlies and people in the state and so on, people in tiny little Party organizations—were let off with slaps and fines and ruined careers and sort of a political reorganization, reimposed political correctnesses, and ideological conformisms to the post-war hour.

The elite of the old Party apparatus were either killed, and many were tortured, there were institutes for their torture and destruction—many which would be used against Communists later on. We had them in Berlin, long denied. They weren't very extensive, but British armies have always used these methods, contrary to the idea that we've never done so.

And so virtually all of the radical non-humanism which is attested against in this particular regime retrospectively was committed, directly and indirectly, by Allied power in the years after 1945 through 1948. The suffering of the Germans, which was extensive, has rarely ever been revealed; the vast majority of people who are alive now have almost no knowledge of it, and rather like other defeated peoples—the white South and the Confederacy in the United States, for example, much of whose history has been consigned to a sort of convenient Orwellian memory hole—few people today know anything about that; or even wish to know.

The irony is that this information is there. If you type into Google "massacres of Germans post 1945"; if you type into Google "German suffering post Second War," masses of material comes up. The problem is not that the material is censored, it's that the masses have been taught that to even look at it is morally evil. And therefore they don't want to look at it, and it's as if it has not occurred, and it's only for archival and specialist interest. It is not where one wishes to put one's gaze.

The revelations about the post-war camps were largely because the Allies took the static photographic cameras of the newsreels of that day to the camps, because they had not to show the world the devastation of the German cities. These beautiful cities all over Germany—north, west, south, and east—that were totally obliterated and totally bulldozed, destroyed more than Grozny by Russian power. Whole cities and towns devastated, and people lived in the rubble for years after 1945.

An old friend of mine, the elitist and non-humanist intellectual Bill Hopkins, served with the RAF after the war as a sort of national serviceman in Hamburg in 1948. His wife's German. They had to pitch the RAF camp *outside* of Hamburg in the summer because of the stench of the bodies under the rubble. Because the smell of the corpses was so nauseating, they couldn't have the camp inside the city.

Eventually, of course, what the Germans would do—and the German economic miracle of the post-war period, which sees the emergence of an economic superpower and a political castrato and pygmy, that is frightened even of its own shadow—in contemporary Germany is rooted in these events. Don't forget many Germans had seen their society smashed to pieces *twice*: in 1918 and in 1945-'46. So it's a sort of double whammy.

Now you know why Germans don't want to put their fighters into Afghanistan and elsewhere. It's not because they're cowards and worriers and are afraid. It's because they, in a sense, have lost the spirit that was destroyed in certain respects in 1945.

The Jewish New York writer Norman Mailer once said that the real victims of the Second World War are the Germans. And not the group, his own group, that is always talked about. And spiritually, someone like Savitri Devi would have agreed with that, because it appears to me as an outsider—despite the Germanic nature of English identity in part—that Germany is self-lost, self-loathing, self-defeating, self-defeated. There's probably no nationality that hates itself more in life than the contemporary Germans.

There are many films about the Left-wing terrorism that emerged out of the '60s and '70s generation, which is seen as a revenge upon the fathers. Waves of hatred of young Germans directed against older and more elderly Germans because of what they did, or more accurately couldn't be said to have done, during the war.

The irony is that Devi is such an extremist that she identifies even with the SS prisoners. Even SS prisoners who weren't in the Waffen-SS, but served in the camps. She regarded those as *heroes* of anti-humanist struggle. People outside time, beyond good and evil, struggling against titanic forces, and going down gloriously and being martyred thereby.

This is essentially a religious view. A powerful and primordial religious view. I see no logical connection, but I sense this. In Shi'a Islam, there's a ceremony where people beat themselves and mutilate their foreheads and this sort of thing, and it's a threnody and a paroxysm. And, in a way, she considers these forms of political movements to be the white equivalent of that. That's how she sees it. The powerful primordial tragedy of the ancient world returned with modern technology in modernity. And that's why, in a sense, her passion for the most hated regime in the twentieth century, as commonly perceived, is primordial and against time.

She went to Germany and distributed handbills almost in a desire to get arrested. A couple of thousand largely [unintelligible] style leaflets of a pro-Axis and pro-restorationist and pro-Hitlerian type, and she was immediately arrested and tried and sentenced to four years, I think. But ultimately served the better part of two under the Allied-controlled area.[3]

Don't forget, the French, the Germans, and the Americans occupied one sector, and the Soviets the other, and they were already splitting into two entities. As the West moved towards the institutionalization of a secondary political class in Germany, led by mild technocratic administrative conservatives like

[3] Savitri was sentenced on April 5, 1949 to three years in prison, but she was released on August 18, 1949 at the request of the Nehru government in India. —Ed.

Adenauer, who erected the post-war set-up dominated by American power.

Don't forget, there's large British bases and even larger American bases in Germany today. Germany is still partly an occupied country that can't entirely be trusted. Even within the EU, even bound in so much, it still can't entirely be trusted, although the West in a way wants a democratic Germany to be strong with them in Iraq and Afghanistan and elsewhere. But Germany is paralyzed and spiritually defeated by what occurred in the aftermath of 1945.

Now, German suffering at the end of the war is not seen by Devi in the way that it normally is. You do sense by liberals you have a sympathy for the other side, such as James Bacque in his books about German suffering at the end of the Second World War. He in many ways is playing a humanist game. It's just he has a new section of victims: German women, German children, people who suffered in the rubble.

In a sense, he feels sorry for them in the way he feels sorry for legless Angolans, or he feels sorry for African AIDS victims, or he feels sorry for the victims of Cortés or for the Haitian earthquake. You see what I mean? It's a new group about which one can have sympathy, and I can write and make a career out of sympathizing for those who were regarded as untouchable before, and I'm a general humanist.

She sees it very differently. She sees it as a suffering and a fire and a threnody which Germans should go through until they can renew themselves again in strength and in glory.

And this leads her in her most famous, infamous, and notorious book, *The Lightning and the Sun*, to essentially engage in the deification of Hitler. A truly extraordinary situation if you consider the mass narrative of the post-war world in the twentieth century. She basically inverts the semiotics. She inverts the narrative of the twentieth century. The greatest villain, the greatest evildoer, the greatest hatemonger, the greatest monster, and she turns him into an avatar of the god Vishnu and says he's divine, and he's beyond human.

Because in the Hindu aristocratic and warrior tradition, there are men of impersonal violence. Titans who walk the

Earth, who are beyond good and evil, and are unrestrained, but whose cruelty and ardor is impersonal, non-material, for idealistic purposes, and is never done for human gain or for their own gain, or for that of their families and their tribes except in the most indirect of ways. So you sense the extremity of her passion in this way.

In some ways, she's synthesizing religious ideas together that were quite new in certain respects and are rooted in her view of nature.

What's the difference between paganism and Christianity? Is it the worship of polytheistic gods? Many pagans actually believe there's one source, and the gods and goddesses are metaphors. Pagans believe everything that exists is divine, in all of the systems. This means that destruction is divine, as well as creation. It also believes that femininity is divine, and therefore there's no problem with the masculine-feminine polarity in all things. There are priestesses in these religions, there are goddesses in these religions, because they're half of what it is to be mortal.

All humans die, go back into eternity, go back into nature, come again. Everything comes again. If we're evolving it's very slow, and on the whole, evolution is the advance of a tiny proportion ahead of the others who can barely keep up.

Now, ethically, most pagan systems are very different. Paganism tends to believe in retributive violence. It tends to believe that if you push me, I'll push you back. It tends to believe even in violence and aggression as the forethought before being attacked oneself. It tends to have an honor-based system whereby morality is perceived hierarchically. So the more noble you are, the more beautiful you are, the more intelligent you are, the more well-proportioned you are, the more knowledgeable you are, the more courage you have, the more favored you are by the gods, the higher you are in a particular hierarchy. This of course has a converse: the uglier you are, the shorter you are, the less well-favored you are, the less courageous[4] you are, the more defective you are, the lower you are

---

[4] Replacing "cowardly." —Ed.

in this particular hierarchy.

This does not mean in accordance with these very ancient precepts that the lower element's cast off or done in or massacred or done down. What it means is that there is a hierarchy in all forms, both within an individual, between individuals, between families of individuals, between groups of individuals — the hierarchy is everywhere, and no one's at the top in any one of the myriad hierarchies.

Notice in all of this discussion, money and finance and how well you've done and how much money you've got, is way, way down in the scale. And mercantile and purely successful forms are not despised because they're part of the whole. Every society has to have a merchant class. Every society has to have a small bit of trade and banking and so on.

But the worship of money and the belief that life is based upon making money is the inverse of her view, and for most of her life she lived as an ascetic. In other words, she lived almost without any property at all and just stayed in the houses of some of the most notorious people on Earth at that time. Some of them living in Egypt, some of them living in Paraguay under General Stroessner, some of them living in Perón's Argentina. Rudel; Johann von Leers, I think, who I believe converted to Islam; Otto Skorzeny, and these sorts of people. They were all her friends, and she lived with them in Madrid, and she visited them in the United States later on.[5] And she travelled all over the world on multiple passports, because she could use Devi, she could use Mukherji, she could use her mother's maiden name, she could use her Greek nationality. Increasingly she became banned from country after country.

After the publication of *The Lightning and the Sun*, I believe she wanted to visit John Tyndall, who's widely known of course. He was essentially the founder of the British National Party. John Tyndall, who was in the National Socialist Movement a long time ago, was an old friend of hers. He used to say,"They just want to keep out a little inoffensive Greek lady

---

[5] Savitri never visited the United States or Paraguay, although she was *en route* to the United States when she died. — Ed.

who 's a friend of mine." But in actual fact it was Savitri Devi really, you know. But that's what he used to say to the BBC when they came asking.

Now, in Germany she was imprisoned, and she wrote a book called *Gold in the Furnace*,[6] about the treatment meted out to her, and to the other prisoners, and the demoralization of the German people post-war. Don't forget the mass of Germans adopted a self-forgetting strategy for the Second [World] War In the '50s, '60s, and early '70s, some of them pricked by the growing Left-wing revolutionism in Germany among student minorities. The older generation blanked it out and concentrated solely on the rebuilding of the society, and everything was rebuilt. If you go to Germany now, you'd never know that American bombers devastated whole sections of cities — although most of the bombing was done by the RAF — deliberately so.

Indeed, as the war progressed, our Air Force became more and more militant, and more and more ferocious. Our crews were told "remember Coventry, remember Southampton." Extraordinary warriorship was shown. In Nietzsche's terms, you never condemn the warrior. The men like Harris and so on, covered with hands of blood, and so on. But show me figures in any nationality that are not like that. David Irving met Harris after the war, of course, and in some ways thought he was a fine warrior, a bulwark, a man who wants to virtually destroy and rend for his people. Not the image the English have of themselves.

Fifty thousand of our air crew died in the air. Unlike the Serbs and the Iraqis, the Germans were able to fight back against this mass terror bombing, and killed an enormous number of the pilots who went over, many of whom didn't survive three to four missions in the air.

But on the ground, hundreds and hundreds of thousands were killed, and incendiaries were deliberately used to create firestorms due to the wind that was created in these cities, in

---

[6] Actually Savitri speaks about her trial an imprisonment in *Defiance*. — Ed.

Hamburg and in Dresden, most famously, which still causes a quiver of conscience in contemporary liberal England and Britain. "Dresden" is a naughty and a dangerous and a dark word, and there is almost a semi-apology on the British lips for Dresden—but not quite.

Stalin ordered Dresden. He ordered Churchill to take these primitive means. There were mass refugees in these cities. He wanted them completely killed and burnt out by the creation of mass firestorms and devastation. The interesting thing is Speer in his autobiography says that if the British and the Americans had concentrated on ball-bearing production, or economic and high-value industrial targets, they could have ended the war from their point of view quicker. But no, the decision was made to devastate urban and suburban and city center areas. Not just a few bombs, but *total* flattening, *total* devastation of these areas. And when areas were not smoldering enough, when the photos were taken, you went back and smashed the area to pieces again, and you put incendiaries on top to make sure it burnt, and good and proper.

When Dresden occurred, there was outrage in the non-aligned world, in Latin America, sympathetic to the Axis of course, because of the hostility, geopolitically, to the United States, and also in the Arab world. And there's an interesting thing that occurred which Irving reveals in his book *Dresden: Apocalypse 1945*—the later and the earlier editions—this is that the cabinet, the war cabinet, which was Tory, Labour, and Liberal, don't forget, tried to force responsibility for Dresden onto the RAF High Command. But they, in their excessive zeal to conduct the war in the air against the Axis, the idea which Orwell uses in *Nineteen Eighty-Four* of Airstrip One, that Britain's an unsinkable aircraft carrier to devastate Europe, flying bomber after bomber from our territory. The RAF were going to be blamed by the political elite. The RAF leadership made the politicians sign a declaration that they had ordered Dresden and that they were responsible for it, because the warriors will not take the responsibility for ordering these things they're enacting on behalf of the political class in most Western societies.

And the interesting thing is that the devastation of Middle Europe, which is part of the current malaise and part of the modern crisis that we all live in, and that exists around us, is the crucial issue for our civilization in the twentieth century. What it's led to is self-hatred and cosmic and spiritual defeat on almost all levels. Caucasians, broadly speaking, are taught to loathe themselves almost more than any other group, and there's a degree to which it all results in these events, in a twentieth-century version of what Joseph Conrad, in relation to the scramble for Africa in the Belgian occupation of the Congo, called "the heart of darkness." The heart of darkness in the twentieth century is these events. And Devi went straight into that heart of darkness by religious-izing, by hypostatizing, by making an absolute of the things which are considered to be the worst elements in the modern West.

The modern West is now defined by tolerance, by inclusion, by egalitarianism, by hostility to everything that those previous governments represented. That is the definition of citizenship. That is the definition of personal morality. That is the definition of modem Britain. The political class and the media class of to-day would say that anyone who does not accord with that is actually a traitor, not to a particular ideology but to humanity, and to the mainstream, and common mean of what it is to be human.

This shows you that many people will not assert themselves if they believe that assertion to be wrong. Millions and millions of our people don't agree with what's happened to this country since 1948, but they feel traumatized about doing anything about it because of the aftermath of these events, and how they've been formed into a narrative in relation to almost everyone who grows up now.

I had a chat once with a 26-year-old who'd been to Hackney, a comprehensive in Hackney where the whites are about fifty percent. I said, "What did you do in history?" He said, "We did black studies and slavery; we did the Holocaust and the Shoah and Western guilt; and we did a bit about British history" — sort of residual third. So increasingly, large parts of Western populations — and it's more acute in Germany than anywhere else and spreads *out* from the center of Europe—grow up with funk, defeat, self-hatred, the belief that one is descended from nationalities that are amoral, that are immoral, that have produced the most Satanic events of the twentieth century. No other nationality feels this way. No other people feels this way.

Putin's partial, complicated, and revisionistic reinterpretation of Stalin is all about making sure that the Russians don't adopt that tack. Even though he massacred millions of Russians, inside Russia he will still be slightly heroicized as a martial leader, whilst allowing Solzhenitsyn's works to be studied at school. What they're doing is dialectical. They're not allowing their past to focus upon them in the way that the Western media would perhaps like them to, and say, "Look at what you did! Look at what you should be responsible for! You should hang your head in shame forever!"

And it's interesting that probably of all the nationalities, there's few Italians indeed who are fundamentally opposed to the government which existed in the '20s and thereafter, who feel about their own nationality and the pitilessness of their own honor and glory, the way that contemporary Germans do. Most of the contemporary Germans I met—apart from hardliners and residual anti-system types, if you like—are traumatized by guilt, live with the guilt in a sort of cosmic way.

The Germans have a strong metaphysical postulate. They're not empiricists and semi-relativists like us. They don't think heuristically. They don't make it up as they go along. A German always wants his theory first, and then he thinks from the theoretical propositions in a sequential way. And if you put before a people the view that they were right to be defeated, and that the firestorms of their cities were in a sense part of their immorality of purpose for which almost semi-divine punishment was meted out—which is some of the cultural register that does exist—you will find that a growing generation, one, two, three generations of people who loathe their own civilization to such a degree that a few of them will take arms against it. Which is what Baader-Meinhof and the other groups were. They were people taking up arms against their own civilization, from within it, in accordance with doctrines that they had been fed in relation to the aftermath of the last war.

Now, Devi's basic political books are *The Lightning and the Sun*, which deals with three historical figures: Genghis Khan, Akhnaton, and Hitler. She sees the one as a man of peace and the Sun, another as a warrior and a killer without any greater idea, and Hitler as a sort of a god and a devil combined. As a sort of superman, outside history. He is against time. He is sort of inhuman. He's considered as something semi-divine.

The irony, of course, is that is how he's perceived in Western culture. The number of films, the number of plays, the number of ideas that feed on him, retrospectively, as a sort of force; as a force of negation, as a force of anti-divinity, because of course, in a dualist system, evil is very powerful, and the idea of the diabolical is extraordinarily provocative and interesting. And he is presented in diabolical colors. Indeed, there is nothing more diabolical. So in a way her configuration, and her spiritual cosmogony, and that which has occurred, are identical in the way that a photographic negative and a photographic image, a positive, is the same image reversed, the one from the other. She has the absolutist view, albeit in reverse, of the contemporary society about him and his dictatorship.

Virtually no one else in the rest of the world who's lived under Mao, who's lived under Ho Chi Minh, who's lived under Choibalsan in Mongolia (Stalin's protégé), who's lived under Stalin, who's lived under Pol Pot—none of them have the view of their own nationality demonically transfigured and embodied by one individual in the way that the Germans do. And in a sense their attitude toward their own re-education and indoctrination post-war is religious. They had a pre-war adoration of him and his regime that was semi-religious. And they have a post-war diabolical instantiation and demonization of the very same things which is almost semi-religious, both ideologically and in its fervor, and in its ability to affect people.

I certainly believe that the West will never revive until these events are internalized and overcome. Nietzsche talks about "self-over-becoming." The idea that you take pain, and loss, and grievance, and agony, and you supplant it, and you rise above it. And you take it into yourself, wash it, and turn it around, and step through it and beyond it. It's a warrior attitude, essentially, applied to civic, mental, and other factors. The only reason that we are, as a culture, in the state that we're in is because of the way in which we think, have been taught to think, and the morality that most of our people have imbibed.

Our people could be incredibly strong, and incredibly militant, if they stepped forward out of the quagmire of moral guilt about events, which is paradoxical now, extend way beyond Germany. The irony is that the entire West has partly indoctrinated itself to feel responsible for things which people in certain nationalities — British nationality for example, Russian nationality (not the same), American nationality — have no physical responsibility for, and even destroyed retrospectively, the governments alleged to be responsible for these actions. So you have this strange situation where the United States has enormous, quasi-religious memorials to the Shoah which are quite theological and sort of theophanic.

I was in Miami about this time last year, and there are enormous memorials to the Shoah in Miami. Enormous memorials! The hand in the center of Miami with the bodies falling from it — which is the Shoah memorial — is as big as a quarter of Trafalgar Square and is a place of *worship*, sort of reverse worship. It's not just a tourist icon and something that's been stuck there. It is a symbol of ontological malevolence in our times before which all must kneel. All know the presence of malevolence and death when they see this. And there's another memorial which we don't see actually, which is actually somewhere else, I think down near the beach, with twisted figures and sort of nautical names on a black sort of plinth, which is rather like the memorial to the Vietnam dead in Washington, DC. And these exist for a purpose. That sort of philo-Semitism and self-hatred is virtually semi-religious.

It's interesting that it's so acute in a Protestant society like the contemporary United States, but maybe it's been concretized in that society, but it exists elsewhere, everywhere. It exists in the minds of the people who defeated Germany. They are responsible as well. It's left national borders and it's become sort of cosmic, and it's what I call the cloud: it's the cloud that appears; the cloud of knowing rather than unknowing to readapt a sort of idealistic religious text. And it falls upon virtually all Caucasians and to a certain extent certain other groups just outside us like a pall. It falls upon us like a miasma, like a sort of moral hectoring and semi-plague. It's only when it's corrosively dealt with that we will revive, because if we remain beholden to this . . .

And there are signs that the onus is beginning to leave us as these events are more and more historicized. You can sense that some of the things made about these events have a shudder running through them. They're not revisionist films in any sense. They're not revisionist books in any sense. But you notice that some of the quasi-religious passion stirred by the Second [World] War are dying as the generation that fought it dies out. More complicated and reflexive and artistically truthful presentations of Germans in struggle during the last war. More complicated presentations of Allied actions during that war. In other words, not presented purely as a crusade against evil.

The truth of the matter is, is that the great unknown guilty consciousness in our own society is we should have made peace in 1941. We should have allowed it. We should have turned towards ourselves and towards our Empire, we should essentially have taken the deal that in a roundabout sort of way he was basically offering us: which is that he dominated Europe and we kept the Empire. After the war, a few figures: A. J. P. Taylor—yes and no; David Irving—yes; Maurice Cowling—yes; Professor Charmley—yes, a few people, most of them historians, not all, have said these things, but no politician will say them. No politician will say them. And yet everything about this society has been semi-blitzed and destroyed as a result of the choices that were made then, and the morality that's been erected upon the nature of the choices that were both made and not made then.

The importance of someone like Savitri Devi is her extremism, because she is unafraid. She was disappointed that she wasn't given the death penalty for distributing these handbills in Germany, because you see, she's a martyr! It's a sensibility that in a sense, people are so far away from now, they can't even begin to understand, essentially.

Robespierre and these Leftists at the end of the eighteenth century had a streak of it. Robespierre was always talking about martyr me, martyr me, if you don't agree. And of course eventually they dragged him to the guillotine, and he went down, and the head went in the basket, and his brother who had a broken jaw from a bullet, and so on, he went down under the basket as well, with Couthon, Saint-Just, and the other terrorists.

But this feeling, that one is even prepared to die for a cause — beyond warriorship, which is partly paid mercenary work now — doesn't exist. It virtually doesn't exist anywhere. It's truly extraordinary, and in some ways it takes an outsider like her: a woman who goes to India, and becomes a Hindu, and rejects Christianity, who's a *fundamentalist* pagan. Notice how many British she's crossed in relation to Western normality just to do all that. It's almost the energy that that sort of arcane and slightly occultistic path of extremity will lead you to, that allows a woman like this to adopt these sorts of positions.

I think the reason why a lot of these elderly SA and SS and Wehrmacht and bureaucratic people who'd served the government and other allies in other countries who felt totally demoralized and totally dispirited and were totally crushed, many of them post-war, many of them were the pariahs. The pariahs of pariahs of post-war life. What they saw in her — and she was an outsider, really, even in relation to them — what they saw in her was somebody who defended them morally. That's why they responded to this little Greek woman in the way that they did. Because she defended them *morally* when they were regarded as the worst people of all, do you see? And that's probably the extraordinary thing: that she affected this sort of ethical reversal. Because what's gone on is more than propaganda.

Enormous propaganda now about Iran in the Western media, you see it everywhere. What are they doing with those plants under the mountains? Are they a threat to us? We need to take action. Neutrality is objective traitorousness. We need to take action. Blair said at the Chilcot Inquiry that any country that worries us, any country that sort of causes us concern, we must *crush it, crush it down* with mass bombing and American power, and we're their auxiliary.

This rather shakes liberals, you know, because people like Blair is a believer. Blair is a believer in this liberal system, and that's why the *taint* of immorality, the *taint* of political Satanism, the *taint* of evil has been projected onto people who have radically European views.

The analytical and psychological school that gentile Europeans like more than Freudianism is Jung's theories because they're more artistic, more reflexive, more appropriate to gentile consciousness. As Freud once said, "He's the most important man in the psychoanalytical movement because he's the only one who isn't a Jew." And Jung's theories involve the idea of the shadow. The shadow is the negation that you project onto the Other. The Other becomes the custodian of all immorality. Not me. *Not* me. The *other*, the one over there, the wretch over there, not me! I admit I'm not a saint. I'm — you know — united. I know what's what! But there, him, them over there. The projection of the shadow and the inability to realize that we all cast a shadow, and therefore that we all have one of our own.

One of the great traumas of the nineteenth and twentieth centuries, of course, is the absence of an alliance between Britain and Germany, which, if it would have occurred, would have changed the whole world, just as the victory of the Confederacy in the Civil War in the United States would have certainly changed the whole world and the one hundred fifty years that we've been through subsequently.

When Joseph Chamberlain was Colonial Secretary in the 1890s, he wanted a treaty or a binding agreement with Germany, so that they would essentially and over time become the *overwhelming* power on the European continent, and they would have to come to concordats with France to one side and Russia to the other, because that's the reality of *Realpolitik*. But we would have our Empire to one side of it. And possibly with the Americans in an isolationist mode, the sort of Charles Lindbergh version of the United States rather than the Bill Clinton version of the United States, the US could have remained a power in the Americas, which is their natural role.

Britain, America keeping to its business, essentially in the Caribbean and the generalized Americas, Germany dominating Europe. No First [World] War, no Second [World] War, and no version of the society that we have now. That was something that was postulated by British leaders like Chamberlain, again an outsider and an establishment radical who comes from the liberals, and yet in some ways he's more energized and more Right-wing than many of the Tories with whom he was associated. If these ideas had prevailed, the present travail would have not occurred.

And Savitri Devi is important to me for two reasons. One is that she says that the people who are thought to be the most immoral on Earth, in contemporary jargon and argot, may not be. And she provides philosophical and theological reasons for that. And even if you don't agree with that—as many of our people would not—there's a secondary position: and that is that the culture of self-hatred and funk and defeat must come to an end.

If you look at many young white people now, they're interested in nature. They're interested in ecology. They're interested in animals, even animal rights, of which she was an early advocate, being a Hindu of course. She didn't believe in using fur. She didn't believe in eating meat, or eggs, or fish. She was absolutist, as Hitler was. All vivisection was banned in Germany, and the most Green and ecological laws were just passed. Business had to obey them. They were just passed. There was no discussion. And they worked around them, you know, as businessmen always do. But *primordial* Green views were passed. Enormous forests were planted around German cities and so on.

The interesting thing is the emergence of the Green movement in post-war Germany, which tacked culturally to the Left. Because Communism can't exist in West Germany, because there's an invidious Communist state in East Germany, so Leftism takes a Green form in West Germany. And yet, Green ideas are not Left-wing. *Deep* Green ideas, as they're called, are *pri-*

mordial and *pagan* (with a small "p") and very, very Right-wing.

She wrote a book called *Impeachment of Man* which is— again, because she's always so extreme—one of the most extreme vegetarian—she wasn't a vegan, technically, but quasi-vegan works—that you could ever imagine.

I remember once, when I was 18, sitting and watching a film called *Animal Auschwitz*, which is a film by the Animal Liberation Front. It's an illegal film; it's an underground film. Animal Liberation Front was formed in relation to a book called *Animal Liberation* by the Jewish university professor from Australia called Peter Singer. Which is a totally other debate, and we won't get into that.

But the interesting thing about the ALF is I think the ALF was founded by Ronnie Lee from Leeds, or he was certainly instrumental in creating it, or one of its leaders, because it was an anarchist thing, they didn't have a structured leadership formally. And he said that fascists or extreme Rightists were welcome in the Animal Liberation Front as long as they didn't bring their politics into it. Which is a sort of strange way of putting it, really. But everyone knows that in those movements, in those alternative and counter-cultural verities, there are interconnected Right-wing ideas.

And one of her most interesting attitudes towards National Socialism is the belief that there are two forms of it. There's the exoteric form that the masses understand, which is a particular group that's responsible for postmodernity, and one doesn't like in an *a priori* way. Certain attitudes toward nature, hierarchy, militarism, extreme patriotism, semi-worship of the state, that the nation and the state are considered to be contiguous, hostility to Modernism in art, Green ideas, and so on. But there is an inner—Those are the views that when they're viewed in a very negative way—the present anti-fascist society has: it's all negative. They don't like persons of color; they don't like homosexuals; they don't like this, they don't like that; they read genesis and disgenesis, da, de da, de da.

She also believes or posits the idea that there as an inner version. And that is the achievement of something that's beyond man as he presently is. And this is the idea of the Superman.

Now, various academics such as Goodrick-Clarke have expatiated at great lengths about the occult roots of National Socialism and pagan and magical ideas, irrationalist ideas, objectivist philosophical ideas which are theological and regarded as irrational by contemporary modernity.

Don't forget, these sorts of notions act upon the will. Bernard Shaw, the Left-wing Nietzschean and playwright at the beginning of the twentieth century and Fabian idealist, said that a man with a crucial idea is worth fifty other men. And essentially that is the fact.

The reason the Islamic world is so strong now, and the reason that some whites, even underneath their hostility, have an attraction to it, is because people are prepared to believe and kill and die for their beliefs. And that gives a power; it gives a power; it gives a resonance.

When Blair says that we're prepared to fight for tolerance — I'm not prepared to fight for tolerance. But I'm prepared to fight for the people that existed on this island before me. And I'm alive now, and I'm a continuation of that. So one is prepared to fight for certain things and not for others. And I think that will, identity, spirit, and idealism in a woman who will be considered to be essentially insane by mainstream modernity — I mean let's not beat about the bush — is very instructive, because in her sort of messianic post-sanity there lies a redemptive element.

I've always been an extremist, ever since I was very young, and that's quite unusual. My father was a bank manager. I came from a very ordinary bourgeois background. When I was 18 he said, "Keep your head down, son. Never get in the papers. Never do anything that will cause any trouble. Never do anything that will cause people to dislike you, and spend your entire life making money." That was the advice I was given. And I'm not demonizing him; he's a representative of thousands and thousands of other people saying exactly the same thing. And I have never believed that that's what life is about. I've never believed that that's what life is about.

Life is about *death*. I'm essentially a religious person in an atheist age. The religions of my society have collapsed. That's why I'm a Nietzschean, you see, because you begin to rebuild from yourself, because there's nothing else left. There's nothing else left. And with somebody as extreme as her—even I don't concur with necessarily all of her views—the power and the purity and the obsessionality of her religious belief in the re-demption of this civilization is very instructive, and very re-vealing, and is a sort of moral dynamite in comparison to eve-rything that's taught in every school and every college and every university now.

I'll leave you on this thought. Remember that film, that French film about the men who carry the nitroglycerine across the desert—*Wages of Fear*—and the slightest bump and the slightest crevice, and there's some tiny pittance of a wage for doing this, you know, for some pitiless boss who never really appears. And they're there in the Sun and the heat and the dust. And the slightest thing can cause the thing to blow up. They've got the courage to go on because they must go on, be-cause to stop is to be defeated by the thing, and it might go off then, anyway. And you keep on going, and you keep on push-ing.

And I personally think that she's a redemptive sort of acid or alkaline solution to reverse it, to everything you've been taught, and everything that your history teacher said to you at pre-A level. And everything you see on the BBC. Her sort of work is like watching the news on the BBC, attacking the TV with a hammer, then attacking the cathode-ray oscilloscope inside the TV—pre-sort of those ones that you hang on the wall—and then seeing that blow up, and then kick the cathode-ray oscilloscope round the garden. And then getting some bof-fin in to reconstitute it in a totally rewired and completely dif-ferent way.

As if the Germans just didn't conquer the Channel Islands but had actually won the war. And you turn on the set again after having smashed it and gone through this extraordinary sort of convoluted process of reorganization. And you sit there, and you watch the news, and there's a bloke in a German uni-form, and you go, "What is going on?" And that's the sort of kinetic, sort of silent film, sort of Eisenstein in reverse that she sort of creates. It's like the coldest of cold baths after liberal wetness and warm-heartedness for so many years. You know, it is a redemptive tonic.

There are various fringe groups about which academics like Goodrick-Clarke make a good career postulating that, you know, the eclipse of the Sun is a new swastika, and there's a Dark Sun, and these groups are out there, and she's their priestess, and she's a source of semi-worship for them, and so on. And if you go on *YouTube* there's pictures of her and accounts of her speeches and writings and so on that call her a Daughter of the Black Sun.

But she is very, very interesting, because she has taken the tiger by the tail and twisted it around. And if you want to morally shock the people who are alive now, don't introduce them to Tarantino's films. Don't introduce them to Sarah Young's pornography. [Introduce them to Savitri Devi, Daughter of the Black Sun.][7]

---

[7] The last words are cut off, but I have provided the gist of the conclusion. —Ed.

JULIUS EVOLA:
THE WORLD'S MOST RIGHT-WING THINKER*

This is the twenty-seventh meeting of the New Right, and we've waited quite a long time to discuss one of the most important thinkers of the radical Right and of a Traditional perspective upon mankind and reality, and that is Baron Julius Evola.

Now, Evola is in some respects to the Right of everybody that we've ever considered in nearly any of these talks, and not in a sort of unprofound or sententious manner. Julius Evola was somebody who rejected purposefully and metaphysically the modern world. Now, what does that mean? It basically means that at the beginning of the last century, Baron Evola, who is a Sicilian baron,[1] decided that there are about four alternatives in relation to modern life for those of a heroic spirit.

One was suicide and to make off with one's self by opening one's veins in the warm bath like Sicilian Mafiosi and Italian cardinals and Sicilian sort of brigands and ancient Romans.

Another was to become a Nietzschean, which for many people in Tradition is a modern version of some, but by no means all, of their ideas, and it's a way of riding the tiger of modernity and dealing with that which exists around us now. Later, people like Evola and other perennial Traditionalists, as we may well call them, became increasingly critical of Nietzsche and regard him as a sort of decadent modern and an active nihilist who has a bit of spirit and vigor, but doesn't really have the real position.

I make things quite clear. I would be regarded by most people as a Nietzschean, and philosophically that's the motivation

---

* This lecture was delivered to the English New Right in London on June 5, 2010. The transcript was made by V. S.
[1] There is no evidence to indicate that Evola was an actual Baron; rather, the title seems to have been an honorific bestowed upon him by his admirers in reference to his aristocratic origins. —Ed.

I've always had since my beginning. That's why parties don't really mean that much to me, because ideas are eternal and ideas and values come back, but movements and the ways and forms that they take and expressions that they have come and go.

Now, moving from the Nietzschean perspective, which of course relates to the great German thinker at the end of the nineteenth century and his active and quasi-existential and volitional view of man, is the idea of foundational religiosity, or primary religious and spiritual purpose. In high philosophy, there are views which dominate everyone around us and modern media and everyone who goes to a tertiary educational college, such as a university, in the Western world. These are modern ideas, which are materialistic and anti-spiritual and aspiritual and anti-religious, or antagonistic to prior religious belief so much so that it's taken as a given that those are the views that one holds. All of the views that have convulsed the Western intelligentsia since the Second European Civil War which ended in 1945, ideas like existentialism and behaviorism and structuralism and so on, are all atheistic and material views. They've been discussed in other meetings. As one goes back slightly, one has various currents of opinion such as Marxism and Freudianism and behaviorism beginning in the late nineteenth century and convulsing much of the twentieth century.

But these are views that an advanced Evolian type perspective rejects. These views are anti-metaphysical and often counter the idea that metaphysics doesn't exist, that it's the school returning of the late Medieval period, what was called the Medieval schoolmen. In some of his books, Evola talks about Heidegger, Martin Heidegger, of course, who got in trouble in the 1930s for his alleged academic sort of positioning in relation to the most controversial regime of modernity. Heidegger, in my opinion, and I've talked about Heidegger before, is a quasi-essentialist to an essentialist thinker. Evola believes he's an existentialist, but that's largely by the by.

These anti-metaphysical views are that which surrounds us. All liberalism, all feminism, all quasi-Marxism, all bourgeois

Marxism, all Cultural Marxism, the extreme Left moderated a bit into the center, high capitalist economics and the return of old liberalism against the Keynesianism which was the soft Marxism that replaced it earlier in the twentieth century . . . All of these ideas are materialistic and atheistic and aspiritual and anti-metaphysical.

You could argue that the heroic Nietzschean dilemma in relation to what's called modernity is a quasi-metaphysical and metaphysically subjectivist view that there are values outside man and outside history that human beings commune with by virtue of the intensity with which they live their own lives. But there is a question mark over, one, the supernatural, and two, whether there is anything beyond and outside man within which those values could be anchored.

So, the idea of an impermanence, the idea of a metaphysical realm which most prior civilizations — indeed, Evola and the Traditionalists would say *all* prior civilizations are based on — is questioned by the Nietzschean compact. It is ultimately, maybe, the beginnings of a very Right-wing modern view, but it is a modernist view. Take it or leave it.

The sort of viewpoint that Evola moved towards, and there was a progression in his early life and spiritual career and intellectual and writing career, is towards what we might call metaphysical objectivism. This is called in present-day language foundationalism or fundamentalism in relation to religiosity. Fundamentalism, like the far Right, are the two areas of culture that can't be assimilated in what exists out there in Praed Street. They're the two things that are outside, and that's why they can never entirely be drawn in.

Now, metaphysical objectivism is the absolute belief in the supernatural, the absolute belief in other states of reality, the absolute belief in gods and goddesses, the absolute belief in one supreme power (monotheism as against polytheism, for example), the absolute belief that certain iterizations, certain forms of language and spiritual culture exist outside man: truth, justice, the meaning of law, purposive or teleological information about how a life should be lived. Most people in Western societies now are so dumbed down and so degraded by almost every aspect of life that nearly *any* philosophical speculation about life is indeterminate and almost completely meaningless. It's a channel which they never turn on.

Now, the type of metaphysical objectivism that Evola postulates as being an anchor for meaning in modern life can take many different forms. One of the great problems many Right-wing or re-foundational or primal movements or tribal movements or nationalistic movements of whatever character have is if there's a religion somewhere behind it — as there often is for many, but not all of the key people involved in such movements and struggles — what form should that be? Everyone knows that culturally, and this is true of a formulation like GRECE or the New Right in France, as soon as you begin to get people of like mind together they will split on whether they're atheist or not, secularists or not, but they are also, on a deeper cultural level, split on whether they're pagan-influenced or Christian. Such divisions always bedevil Right-wing cultural and metapolitical groups.

The way that the Evolian Tradition looks at this is to engage in what's called perennialism. This is the inherent intellectual and ideological and theological idea that there are certain key truths in all of the major faiths. All of those faiths that have survived, that are recorded, that have come down to us, even their pale antecedents, even those dissident, deviant, and would-be heretical elements of them that have been removed, in all of them can be seen a shard of the perspectival truth that these particular traditions could be said to manifest. Beneath this, of course, is the ethnic and racial idea that people in different groups within mankind as a body perceive reality differently, experience it differently, have different intellectual and linguistic responses to it, and form different cults, different myths, different religions because they are physically constituted in a manner that leads to such differentiation.

This can lead among certain perennialists to a sort of universalism at times, almost a neo-liberalism occasionally, where *all* cultures are of value, where *all* are "interesting," where *all* are slightly interchangeable. But given that danger, the advantage for a deeply religious mind of the perennial tradition is to avoid the sectarianism and negative puritanism which is inevitably part and parcel of building up large religious structures.

As always, a thinker like Evola proceeds from the individual and goes to the individual. This can give thinking of this sort a slightly unreal aspect for many people. Where are the masses? Where is the democratic majority? Where is the BBC vote that decides? The truth is Evola's not concerned with the BBC vote. He's not concerned with the masses. He regards the masses, and the sort of theorists who go along with him regard the masses, as sacks of potatoes to be moved about. His thinking is completely anti-democratic, Machiavellian to a degree, and even manipulative of the masses as long as it's done within an order of Tradition within which all have a part.

Evola dates the decline of modernity from, in a sense, the end of the Middle Ages and the beginning of the Renaissance. But many thinkers of a similar sort date the slide at other times. Evola's a Catholic, and once asked about his religious peculiarity or particularism, he said, "I'm a Catholic pagan," which is a deeply truthful remark, dialectically. I am not a Christian, but if you look at it from the outside, the core or *ur* part of Christianity is obviously Roman Catholicism, even though I was technically brought up in the Protestant sort of forcing house of Anglicanism. A wet sheet religion if ever there was one. But Anglicanism, of course, is a syncretic religion. It's a politically created religion. A bit Catholic, a bit Protestant, but not too much, and with a liberal clerisy at the top that's partly Protestant-oriented within it and exists to manage the thing.

One of the truthful, although this is *en passant*, asides that can be made about Anglicanism, and the reason why it's been supported even today through state establishmentarianism when virtually no one attends these churches at all except the odd old lady and immigrants from the Third World, is that it's a way of damming up some of the extremism that does lurk in religion. Religion is a very dangerous formulation, as the modern world is beginning to understand.

I remember Robin Cook, who was a minister who opposed the Iraq War and so on, and died on a Scottish mountain, all that obsessive walking when one's thin and redheaded can lead to undue coronaries, but Cook once said — and he's a son of the manse, like most of these Scottish politicians are, in other words, he comes from a Calvinist background to a degree — he said that in his early life, he thought with the general Marxist and Freudian conundrums that religion was over. And now towards the end of his life, this is just before he died, he said, "The dark, clammy, icy hand of religiosity," in all sorts of systems, "is rising again, and secular Leftists like us" — he's speaking of himself and those who believe in his viewpoint — "are feeling the winds of this force coming from the side and from behind [them]." And it's a force that they don't like.

I personally believe, as with Evola, that people are hardwired for faith. Maybe one in ten have no need of it at all. But for most people, it's a *requirement*. The depth of the belief, the knowledge that goes into the belief, the system they come out of, is slightly incidental. But man needs emotional truths. George Bernard Shaw once said, "The one man with belief is worth fifty men who don't have any," and it's quite true that all of the leaders of great movements and those that imposed their will upon destiny inside and outside of particular countries have considerable and transcendent beliefs, philosophical, quasi-philosophical, religious, semi-religious, philosophical melded into religious, and vice versa. Without the belief that there's something above you and before you and beyond you and behind you that leads to that which is above you, we seem as a species content to slough down into the lowest common denominator, the lowest possible level.

Evola and those who think like him believe that this is the lowest age that mankind has ever experienced, despite its technological abundance, despite its extraordinary array of technological devices that even in an upper pub room in central west London you can see around you. It is also true, and this is one of the complications with these sorts of beliefs, that some of the methodologies that have led to this plasma screen behind me would actually be denied by elements of some of the religiosity that people like him would put forward, but that's one of the conundrums about epistemology, about what you mean by meaning, which lurks in these types of theories.

The interesting thing about these beliefs is that they're primal. Turn on the television, turn on the radio, the World Cup is just about to begin. Everywhere there is trivia. Everywhere there is celebration of the majority. Everywhere there is celebration of the desire for us all to embrace and become one world, one world together. I met somebody recently who said, "I don't want to be English. I don't want to be British. England's a puddle," he said. "I want to step out. I want to be a citizen of the world! I don't want to have a race. I don't want to have a kind. I don't want to have a group . . . even a class! I don't want to come from anywhere. I want to be on this planet! This planet is my home!" Well, my view is that sort of fake universality . . . Maybe you should get him one of these little dinky rockets and fire himself off into some other firmament, because this is the home that we have and know. And the only reason that we can define it as such is by virtue of the diversity of what exists upon it. But the number of people who wish to retain that diversity and the pregnant meanings within it seem to get smaller and smaller with each generation.

The politicians that we have now are managers of a social system. It's quite clear that we do not have three ruling parties, but one party with three wings, the nature of which are interchangeable in relation to gender, where you come from in the country, class, background, how you were educated, and whether you arrived in the country as a newcomer in the last forty to fifty years or not.

Now, Evola's step back from what has made the modern world leads to certain radical conclusions about it which are spiritually and politically aristocratic. Most people are only aware of the Left-Right split as it relates to a pre-immigration, slightly organic society where social class was the basis for political alignment. Bourgeois center Right: conservatism of some sort. Center Left: Labour, social democratic, trade unionist, and so on. Now we have a racial intermingling that complicates even that division. The distinction between the aristocratic and upper-class attitude and the bourgeois attitude, which is as pronounced as any Left-Right split between the proletariat and the bourgeoisie, is that which Evola advocates.

Evola believes, in some respects, in masters and slaves, or certainly serfs. He believes that the merchant and those who deal purely with economics have to be subordinated to politics, to higher politics, to metapolitics, to military struggle. He believes that the warrior and the religious leader and the farmer and the intellectual/scholar/craftsman/artist are uniquely superior to those that make money, and nearly all of Evola's views are in some ways a form of aristocraticism, in a way.

If you look at all of the sports that he favors—fencing, mountaineering—they all involve lone individuals who prepare themselves for a task which is usually dangerous and which can usually result (mountaineering, for example, and his book *Meditations on the Peaks*) in annihilation, if you go wrong, but creates an extraordinary and ecstatic sense of self-overbecoming if you conquer K2, the Peruvian mountains, the Eiger, Mount Everest, and so on. And even in the more populist forms of mountaineering, the sort of beard and upper-middle-class, Chris Bonington, sort of cheery mountaineering as you might call it, there is a streak of aristocratic, devil may care, and Byronic license. The bourgeois view is, "Why do that!? It's dangerous. It's pitiless. You could be hurt and injured! There is no profit. It serves no higher reason than itself." For Evola, the reason and the purpose *is* the reason to do it. It is the stages that you go through and the mental states you get into as you prepare, and you execute a task which is dangerous, and the same analogy can be extended to martial combat, the same analogy can be extended to sports like ancient wrestling.

Modern wrestling is a circus, of course, where the outcome is largely decided by the middlemen who negotiate the bouts between clowns, who can still damage each other very severely. But ancient wrestling was a bout that ended very quickly and was essentially religious, which is why the area that they wrestled in was purified with salt in most of the major traditions, and so on.

Fencing: take away the protective gloves and gear and you have gladiatorial combat between people who are virtually on the brink of life and death. It's only one step removed from Olympic fencing. Notice that in the contemporary Olympics, a movement that was founded in modernity on the Grecian ideal, nearly always founded by aristocrats, all of the early victors in shooting and fencing and all these early sports are aristocrats. Of course, the early Olympics have their funny side. Many of the female athletes that won the early Olympic competitions were transsexuals. Of course, medical checks were instituted to prevent hermaphrodites and people of diverse genders and that sort of thing from competing in these competitions. But the individualistic sports in a mass age have been disprivileged and are largely regarded as strange wonderland sports that the masses only flip channels over in relation to the Olympics.

For a man like Evola and for the sensibility which he represents, things like sport are not a diversion. They are targets for initiation in relation to processes of understanding about self, the Other, and life that transcend the moment. So, one bout leads to another, leads to another moment of skill. It's as if these moments, which most people always try to avoid rather than engage upon, are in slow motion. The whole point of Evola's attitude towards these and other matters is to go beyond that which exists in a manner which is upwards and transcendent in its portending direction.

This is a society which always looks downwards. "What will other people think? What will one's neighbors think? What will people out there think? What will all this BBC audience think? What do the masses, Left, Right, center, pressing their buttons on panels and consoles think?" The sort of Evolian response is that what they think is of no importance, and they ought to think what the aristocrats of the world, in accordance with the traditions, which are largely religious, out of which their social order comes, thinks. You can understand that this is an attitude which is not endeared, this type of thinking, to contemporary pundits and to the world as it now is.

It's also inevitable that when Evola's books were published, they would enter the English-speaking world via the occult, via mysticism, via various types of initiated and individualistic religiosity. The whole point about the Western occult, whether one believes in the literal formulation that these people spout or whether one believes in it metaphorically and quasi-subjectively, is that it's an individualistic form of religiosity. In simple terms, mass religion involves a small clerisy or priesthood in the old Catholic sense up there, and the laity are down there, and it's in Medieval Latin, it's slightly mysterious, you partly understand it if you're grammar school educated, otherwise you don't, it's mysterious and semi-initiated, but you don't really know, the mystery is part of the wonder of the thing, you're looking up at them and they've got their back to you, and they're looking up further, further beyond them towards the divine as they perceive it. Now, that's a traditional form of mass religiosity, if you like.

But the type of religiosity with which he was concerned was individualistic and voltaic. It was essentially the idea that everyone in a small group is a priest. Sometimes there's a priest and a warrior combined. One of the many scandals that we have in modernity is crimes that are committed by members of various religious groups and organizations. Many Traditionalist-minded people believe that the reporting of these crimes in the mass media is deliberately exaggerated in order to demonize any retrospectively traditional elements of a prior and metaphysically conservative type in the society.

But if one looks at it another way—and one of the things about Evola is the creativeness of the aristocratic mind that looks at essentially centrist and bourgeois problems in a completely different perspective—he would say about those sorts of scandals, which I won't belabor people with because everyone knows about them, that it's the absence of the dialectic between the priest, somebody who believes in something, somebody who believes in a philosophy that isn't just theirs and therefore relates to a society and relates to a continuing generic tradition out of which they come . . . Most contemporary philosophers are "just my view." "Just my view as a tiny little atom." Rather than my view as something that's concentric and links me to something larger and which therefore can be socially efficacious. But from an Evolian perspective, the absence of

the warrior or the martial and soldierly traditions and its interconnection with belief and the individual who believes is the
reason for decadence or deconstruction or devilment or decay
in these religious organizations. In his way of looking at things,
there's a seamlessness between the poet-artist, the warrior, and
the religious believer. They are different formulations of the
same sort of thing, because they're always looking upwards
and, in a way, are deeply individualistic and egotistical but
transcend that, because the concentration on one's self or one's
own thinking, one's own feeling, one's own concerns, one's
own attitude towards this mountain, this woman, this fight,
this text is conditioned by that which you come out of and
move towards.

Evola doesn't believe in progress, nor does the Tradition
that he comes out of. They don't believe in scientific progress.
They don't believe in evolution. But his anti-evolutionism is
strange and interesting. It's got almost nothing to do with crea-
tionism and, if you like, the Evangelical politics of certain parts
of what you might call the Puritan American Right, for example. His attitude is a reverse attitude, which in a strange way is
an involuntary and inegalitarian way of looking at the same
issue. His view is that the apes are descended from us as we go
upwards, rather than we are descended from them as we leave
them in their simian animalism. So, in a way, it's actually a re-
formulation of the same idea, but looking upwards and always
seeing, if you like, the snobbish, the aristocratic, the prevailing,
the over-arching view rather than viewing the thing from a
mass, generic, and middling perspective which *includes* people.

Tony Blair says the worst vice anyone can have is to be in-
tolerant. It's to be exclusive. It's to exclude people. "The nature
of Britishness is inclusion," when, of course, the nature of any
group identity is exclusion, and who is on the boundary and
who can be allowed in and the subtleties and grains of difference that exist between one excluded group and another,
where one tendency of man ends and another begins. Evola
believes, in a very controversial way, that decline is morphic
and spiritual combined. In other words, races of man have a
spiritual dimension, have a higher emotional dimension, have

a psychological dimension, but never forget that Evola is not a Nietzschean. He is not somebody who believes it's all at this level. He believes that the gods speak to man directly and indirectly and the civilizations that we come out of are based essentially on religious premises.

Moderns who sneer at these sorts of attitudes, of course, forget that virtually every civilization that mankind has ever had until relatively recently, and in every civilization there are documents and artifacts which are included in the storehouse of the British Museum just over there in central London, were religiously and theologically based. It's only really in a post-Enlightenment, Scottish Enlightenment, English Enlightenment, French Enlightenment, eighteenth-century-plus sort of a way that the secularization of Western Europe rivals the rest of the planet. Further east in Europe, less of it. Further south in Europe, a bit less of it. Religiosity on most of the other continents of the Earth is still a primary force, but Evola would despise the sort of religiosity that prevails there because he would see in it broken-down thinking, syncretism—the people who would say he would be in favor of contemporary Saudi Arabia, for example, would probably be sorely disappointed. He would see under the religious police, under the strict observance of this or that rule, American satellite dishes and modern devices and that which is external, in relation to modernity, and which is being internally accepted. So, Evola was always the critic, if you like, and always on the outside.

Now, his career is quite complicated, because when he was a very young man, he fought in the First World War on the Italian side. They, of course, fought on the "Western" or Allied side in that war, as is often forgotten. There are some extraordinary photos of him on the Internet in these goggles and these helmets looking extraordinarily fascistic, and that movement hadn't even really been created then, you know. He looks like that in a D'Annunzian-type way, stylistically, even before the gesture itself.

Evola, of course, partly disapproved of Fascism and National Socialism even though he became very heavily implicated and/or involved in both of them, because in his view they weren't Right-wing enough! They weren't Traditional enough. They weren't organic enough. They weren't extreme enough. Evola is probably the only thinker in the twentieth century who has written a slim volume criticizing National Socialism from the Right, not from any point to the Left. He only aligned with these movements because they forced modernity to question itself and because they were anti-democratic and because they were ferocious and desired morally and semi-theologically — because few, including liberal critics, would deny that there was a semi-theological insistence to most of the radical European movements, even of the Left but certainly of the Right, in the first half of the last century. And Evola saw in these movements a chance, but no more, which is why he flirted with them, why he wrote for Fascist magazines in Italy, why he went to colleges run by Himmler's SS in Germany, why he was disapproved of by them, why he had sympathizers, Ernst Jünger-like, in the Party who protected him, why he was allowed to write with a degree of freedom whilst giving a degree of loyalist obeisance to these structures and yet, at the same time, to remain outside them. The question has to be raised whether Evola's philosophy is consonant with the creation of a society or whether it will become, if you like, a spirited individualism.

Evola was also involved in the beginning of his career in one of the most radical modernist movements of the twentieth century: Dadaism in Italy. He produced some Dadaist paintings. Now this, superficially, looks quite extraordinary, but of course there was a strong interconnection between certain early modernisms and fascistic ideologies. The reason that he became involved in Dadaism is quite interesting, and, of all things, there is a talk on *YouTube* that lasts four-and-a-half minutes in which Evola is an old man explicating why he was involved. He says the reason we got involved in these movements was to attack the bourgeoisie, was to attack the middle class, and was to attack middle class sensibility and sentimentality. The extraordinary radical anti-system nature of many radical Right ideas, which is hidden in more moderate and populist variants, comes out staring at you full in the face in people like Evola. Many fascistic and radical movements of the Right, of course, were peopled by adventurers and outsiders and quasi-artists and demi-criminals and religious mystics and madmen and people who were outside of the grain of mainstream life, particularly people who were socialized by the Great War, which many of them experienced as a revolution.

Wyndham Lewis, who was strongly drawn aesthetically to modernism and politically to various forms of fascism, and was a personal friend of Sir Oswald Mosley, once said that for us, the First [World] War was a revolution, it wasn't a war. We saw killing on a truly industrial scale. We saw the industrialization of slaughter.

One of the interesting ironies of the Evolian, and in some ways Ernst Jünger's, position about war is that, although thinkers like them are regarded by pacifists and liberal humanists and feminists as warmongers, there is a distaste for mass war in Jünger and Evola and the others, because it's the war of the ants, the war of the masses in blood and dung and soil and gore. There is nothing chivalric about a man being torn to pieces by a helicopter gunship when he doesn't even have a chance to get his Armalite into the air.

Evola would prefer the doctrine of the champion. You know, when two Medieval armies meet, and one enormous, hulking man comes out of one army, in full regalia trained in martial splendor and arts, as a previous speaker discussed in relation to the Norse tradition, and another champion emerges, and they fight for a limited objective that leaves civilization intact on either side. But the one that is defeated will obviously pay dues to the other.

Now, this shows the extremely sort of Byronic, individualistic, and aristocratic spirit that lurks in Evola's formulations. The way that his works have come down to us, of course, is the way that he lived his life and the books that he wrote. It's interesting that the Anglo-Saxon world has received his literature through translations by mystic and occultistic publishers in the United States: about Tantra, about Buddhism, about Japanese warrior castes and traditions, about the Holy Grail, about Greco-Roman, high Christian, pagan, and post-pagan Europeanist and other traditions.

Another radicalism about Evola is his total unstuffiness and absence of prudery in dealings with sex. Evola wrote a book called *Metaphysics of Sex*. He regards sexuality as a primal biological instantiation through which the races of man are renewed and replaced. But at the same time, he regarded it as one of the primary human acts of great energy and force that has to be channeled, has to be made use of, has to be transcended in and of itself. You have this odd commitment to Tantra, which is a sort of erotic extremism of occultic sex, and a total opposition to pornography. Why? Because the one involves the commercialization of sex, the one involves money interrelated with sexuality. From this purely sort of primal perspective, unless a marriage is arranged between dynastic states or groups for particular statal purposes, which is fine, money has almost nothing to do with these areas of life.

The disprivileging of money as the basis of everything and the belief that the society that we have now is the result of the fact that every politician in all of the parties represented in the major assemblies, including radical Right parties essentially of a populist hue, believe in *Homo economicus*. They believe that man is an economic integer and nothing else matters. Immigration? It's good for the economy, don't you know? Mass movements of capital around the world at the flick of a button on a screen in exchanges all around the globe, particularly in the Far East now, but also ubiquitously? It's good for the economy! Everything is based upon the freeing of people from prior forms of alleged servitude due to economic enhancement. The sort of doctrines Evola holds are not neo-Medieval, nor are they a desire to return to the ancient world with certain modern technologies. In some ways, they are a return to the verities that existed before the modern world was created.

One of the most substantial critiques of this type of thinking is the belief that the modern world is inevitable, that all cultures and races will modernize and are doing so at a great rate of knots, that skyscrapers and enormous megalopolic cities are being thrust up in the Andes and the Far East and even client, Chinese-built ones will emerge in Africa and elsewhere, and that it would be onwards and upwards forever in relation to what we have now. There are grotesque problems with that, of course, because to give every human on this planet irrespective of race, kinship, clime, and culture a middle-American lifestyle, you will need three planets, eight planets, ten planets, or you may need them, in order to give them that middle-American feeling: the three satellite dishes, the condominium, the three Chelsea tractors outside on the driveway, the multiple channel TV, and so on. To give every African that, we will need many, many planets and many, many times the economic wherewithal that we have even at the moment.

The interesting thing about Evola is that many issues that convulse people today—famine in the Third World, war in the Congo, HIV/AIDS—he would say, "Well, they're interesting, of course, because they're things that are going on, and everything has a meaning even beyond itself." But ultimately, they're unimportant. The number of humans on the Earth doesn't matter to his type of thinking. Pain and suffering does not matter in accordance with his type of thinking. Indeed, he welcomes them as part of the plenitude of life, because life begins in pain and ends in pain, and most people live their entire life in denial of the fact that life is circular, as his philosophical tradition believes the world is and meaning is. There is progression round the circle, but there is decline, and decline and death are part of an endless process of will and becoming.

It is essentially, and in a very cardinal way, a religious view of life, but also a metaphysically pessimistic and conservative view of life in a profound way that the conservatism of contemporary liberal Tories like Cameron would not even begin to understand. To a man like him, theories of Evola's sort are lunacy, quite literally, the return to the Dark Ages, the return to the Middle Ages, quasi-justifications of slavery, quasi-justifications of the Waffen SS. This is what Cameron or his colleagues on the front bench and his even more liberal colleagues on the same front bench would say about these sorts of ideas.

But the irony is that three hundred to four hundred years ago, most civilized structures on Earth were based on these ideas, that even the modern ones that replaced them are based upon the contravention of these sorts of ideas, which means they realized they were real enough to rebel against in the first instance. And it's also true that even in the high point of modernity, post-modernity, hypermodern reality, all the phrases that are used, when a war occurs, when the planes go into the towers in New York, when the helicopter gunships stream over Arabian sands, you suddenly see a slippage in the liberal verities and in the materialism and in some of the ideas which are used to justify these sorts of things. Not much of a slippage, but you suddenly see a slippage, what occultists and mystics call a "rending of the veil," a ripping of the veil of illusion between life and death.

What life is really about. Is life really about shopping? Is life really about making more and more money? Is life really about bourgeois status, when one already has enough to live on? Is life really about eating yourself to death? These are the sorts of things that Evola's viewpoint pushes before people, which is why the majority will always push it away.

His political texts are essentially *Revolt Against the Modern World*, *Men Among the Ruins,* and *Ride the Tiger*, which explore the nature of a man who is born now when most of the prior traditions of his culture and his civilization have collapsed. The decivilization of man, the fact that Western cities have turned into Third-World [unintelligible] sort of zones, the fact that semi-criminality is endemic, the fact that when you go into a street graffiti is there, rap music blares from a passing car, twenty percent, forty percent of the street has no relationship to you aesthetically or ethnically or racially or culturally. Evola would see this as part of the inevitable climate of decline and spiraling downwards towards matter, which is intentional and volitional.

The most controversial area of Evola is when he begins to unpick and reformulate many classic propositionalisms of what might be called the "Old Right" to determine what has occurred and why. Evola is essentially, although he began in a more subjectivist and changeable mood, a deeply religious and aristocratic man. This means there is always a reason. Liberals believe that everything is a confusion and everything is contingent upon itself and everything is an accident waiting to happen. But like Christ in the New Testament, who believes that when two birds fall to the ground, the father is aware, Evola believes that there is always a purpose and a reason. Evola believes that civilizations are collapsing in on themselves and tearing themselves apart internally for reasons that are pushed by elites and by forces which are manifest within them that will that desire. The endless atoms and causal moments in the chains may not know of that which is coming, that which is non-volitional, that which is partly pre-programmed. But he believes that these tendencies of mass servitude, mass death, mass proletarianization spiritually, mass plebeianism, mass social welfare, mass social democracy, are *willed*, that the destructivity of prior cultural orders is willed and is definite, and certain racial groups are *used* to facilitate that destruction, and that other groups use them in order to achieve it.

He believes in an aristocracy of man, because he believes everything is hierarchical. There was an interesting moment in a by-election in East London or eastern London just recently when the chairman of the party that I used to be in a while ago was asked by a woman of Afro-Caribbean ancestry, "Are we equal with you?" The media's there, you know. Twenty cameras are upon this individual, and therefore, given the logic and the paradigm that he is in, he said, "Yes." He would probably want to say, "Yes, but . . . ," but the media has gone on because it's got the required answer. Indeed, a lot of media investigation now is asking a politician to affirm their correctness before a prior methodological statement, and woe betide any of them if they show the slightest backsliding on any issue about which they should be progressive.

Evola's answer — who can put words in the mouth of somebody who died a while back? — but the answer of his type of thinking would be that that woman is unequal in relation to a black writer like Wole Soyinka, who is a Nigerian who's from the Yoruba tribe and won the Nobel Prize. Is he worthy of winning the Nobel Prize? Was he given the prize in the 1990s because it was fashionable to do? Rabindranath Tagore, the great Indian writer and Brahmin and higher-caste type, won it in 1913. Probably wasn't too much political correctness then, but there was probably a bit even then. The Evolian answer is that she is not equal in relation to Soyinka, and Soyinka is not equal in relation to Chaucer or Defoe or Shakespeare or Voltaire or Dante or Tolstoy or Dostoevsky or Wagner, that everything is unequal and that everything is hierarchical and that there's a hierarchy within an individual and between individuals and between groups of individuals, because everything is looking upwards and everything has a different purpose in life.

This means that those who are at the middle and at the bottom of an ethnicity, of a social order, of a gender, of a prior historical dispensation, should not be lonely, in his way of looking at things, or afraid or rebellious or full of alienation and fear, because everyone has a role within a hierarchy and people can move to a degree, although his viewpoint is essentially aristocratic and not meritocratic. A man like Nietzsche, who Bertrand Russell once condemned as advocating an aristocracy when he was not born in it or anywhere near it, a man like him would be accepted, but never completely accepted by an aristocratic caste. Things that are regarded as hopelessly naïve and snobbish now, Evola regards as just due form.

What is the worst thing in the world at the present time, according to Sky News? Probably discrimination. Discrimination of one sort or another. Evola would believe that discrimination is the taxonomy of an aristocratic sensibility. One reaches for a piece of cake, one discriminates. One has an arranged marriage with another member of the Sicilian nobility, one discriminates. One reaches for a sword to do down a bounder that one wishes to beat with the flat of the blade, one discriminates between the weapon and the object of the rage, which is itself indifferent because it sees something beyond even itself. These are views, of course, which the majority of people will find cold, chilling, brutal, eagle-like, beyond almost their conception. Almost forms of insanity, in actual fact, in relation to what is today regarded as normal or moral or even human. They are partly inhuman ideas, in some ways, but they are ideas that most aristocracies and most warrior castes have had for most forms of human history.

Evola's books are now widely available to those who wish to read them. The great conundrum of his work is, does it portend to an asceticism? In other words, if the era of destruction, which is the Kali Yuga on the ideology which he puts forward, which is the Hindu age of destruction where everything is broken and everything is melded together prior to decomposition, which will feed a universal rebirth at a future time, because mankind is seasonal in relation to Spengler's view of the world, where his view of history is compared to plants and botany to give it some sort of methodology, some sort of structure.

Don't forget, these are nineteenth century and early twentieth century ideas. No history don, or hardly any history don, today believes history has a meaning. Carlyle believed that the sort of deistic nature of history impinged upon the decadence of the French royalist elite and it led to the Revolution because they didn't superintend France properly. He sort of believed in his Protestant, thundering way from the pulpit of his study in the mid-nineteenth century that the French Revolution was an outcome that was partly deserved by a failing aristocracy. In other words, history had a meaning. It had a purpose. Nobody believes history has a meaning or a purpose. Certain antifascists would say Stalingrad had a purpose, but they forget that the Red Army shot sixteen to eighteen thousand of their own men, and the commissars stood eighteen feet behind the lines. They shot an army of their own men in order to win that battle, just as secret police in the Third World cut off the ears and cut out the tongues of any who retreat in battle before they send them back to their villages.

Would Evola approve of that? He would probably say, if it was done individualistically or as a matter of revenge or of rage, it's dependent upon circumstances, but to do it in a mass-oriented way — mass camps, mass sirens, the totalitarian response particularly of Communism, the reduction of everything to the lowest common denominator so all can be free in a sort of pig-like uniformity — he would consider that really to be death and to be fought against.

Evola is extraordinarily controversial because there is an area in his thinking, particularly in relation to the Islamic world, that leads almost to the justification, as certain liberal critics say, of forms of religious terrorism. He never *quite* advocates that, but it's quite clear his loathing of the modern world is such, and his nuanced appreciation of the Islamic concept of *jihad*, where you fight within yourself against doubt and fight externally in a quasi-pagan and masculine way against the enemy that is without you, has a resonance that chimes with certain extremist religious people who basically want to blow the modern world up.

So, Evola is, as I say in my title, one of the world's most Right-wing, certainly most elitist, thinkers. The interesting thing about him is that everything always looks upwards, even his doctrine of race.

You find in many racialistic movements a sort of socialism, that if you are of my ethnicity you're "all right," as if possession of a certain melanin skin content or absence of same is all that the thing was about. When Norman Tebbit says that the British National Party is old Labour plus allied racialism, there is always a streak of truth to such viewpoints. Evola doesn't believe in that.

Evola believes that race is spiritual as well as physical. If a man comes to you and says, "Oh, I'm white! You should be looking after me, mate!" he would say what is your intellect, what is your quality, what is your moral sense, what do you know about your civilization, how far are you prepared to fight for it, what pain can you endure, have you had understanding of death in your family and in life, are you a mature and profound human being or are you part of the limitless universality, although you were born in a particular group which I respect and come from myself? That's the sort of principle he would have.

Now, that is an attitude of revolutionary snobbery in a way, but it's snobbery based upon ideas of character. And in the end, as we know, politically, character is a fundamentally important thing. And the absence of it, particularly in quasi-authoritarian movements, is poisonous because people once in place cannot be removed except by the most radical of means. So, there is a degree to which leadership is all-important.

Look at an army. An army is not a gang of thugs, but it can easily become one. An army can easily become a rabble, but armies are controlled by hierarchies of force, the nature of which is partly impalpable. Each squad has a natural leader. Each squad has its non-commissioned officer. Each squad has an officer above them. In real armies, German, British armies of the past, if one officer goes down, somebody replaces them from lower down, assumes immediately the responsibility that goes with that role. Even if all the officers are gone and all the non-commissioned officers, the natural leader, one of the five percent — most behavioral anthropologists believe that one in twenty of all people have leadership criteria — can step forward in a moment of crisis and are looked to by the others, because they provide meaning and order and hierarchy in a moment of stress.

Have you ever noticed that when people undergo disaster or when they're in difficulties, they look for help, but they also look for people to lead them out of it? Leaders are never liked, because it's sort of lonely at the top, but leadership is probably like the desire to believe in something beyond yourself. It's in-born. And while the principle of leadership remains, where in even democratic societies leaders are required in order to ener-gize the democratic masses . . .

Don't forget, most of the Caesarisms of modernity are Red forms of Caesarism, forms of extreme authoritarianism and even pitilessness, all in the name of the people, all raised in the name of the masses and their glory and their freedom, their liberty and their equality. When *Forbes* magazine says that the Castro family's wealth in Communist Cuba is seventy million US dollars, when it calls them Communist princes . . . Don't forget, an ordinary man in Cuba could be in prison for owning his own plumbing business. When you realize that these peo-ple are princelings of reversal, you sense that some of the hier-archies, although they wear different names and different forms, are occurring in an entropic phase or in a culture of de-cay, do relate to many of Evola's ideas even in reversal. He would say this is because these ideas are eternal and are peren-nial and will out in the end.

The traditional political Right-wing criticism of these sorts of ideas is that they're purely philosophical, they relate to individuals and their lives, they tend to Hermeticism and the ascetic view that a learned spiritual man, a man of some substance, can go off and live by himself and the rest can rot down to nothing and who cares. They say that they feed a sort of post-aristocratic misanthropy.

Look at our own aristocracy. They probably lost power in about 1912. They were never shot like in the Soviet Union, they were never beheaded like in revolutionary France of two hundred years before. But they have lost everything, in a way, because their function has been taken from them, hasn't it? The reason for those schools, the reason they were bred in the first place, the reason for all their privileges and so on, has been taken away. The fascination with the Lord Lucan case in the '70s, the sort of decline of that class, you know. He listens to Hitler's speeches at Oxford, beats the nanny to death, not even get the right woman in the basement. This sort of thing. Can't even get *that* right! You know? Couldn't even get the crime right! You know? It's the decline of a class, isn't it? You know, going down, and *knowing* they've gone down as well. It's sort of Oswald Mosley's son enjoys being dressed up as a woman and spanked, and his son's just died of a heroin overdose. And yet Oswald Mosley is in that family chain. You don't really need to really think that there is a sort of efflorescence there. It's a bit unfair on that family and so on.

But don't forget, this was a class that was born to pitilessness and rule. This was a class that identified with eagles. That's why they put them on their shields and on their ties and on their schools. And now look at them.

But, of course, they have in a sense joined the rest, haven't they? They've joined the mass. And what they once were no longer matters. Cameron sums it up in a strange sort of way. Traditionally, since the 1960s, the Tories have always elected pushy, middle-class people with whom the mass of their electoral support can identify.

It was always said Douglas-Home would be the last of the old breed. He was premier when I was born. He would be the last of the old breed that would survive and thrive. When asked about unemployment in 1961, Douglas-Home said, "There's room for a second gamekeeper on my estate." And people said he was out of touch. Out of touch! And he *was* out of touch! Let's face it. But he thought that was a quite commodious and moral answer, you see.

Cameron is strange because all of the ease – the ease before the camera, the ease before people, no notes, look at me, not a trembling lip – all of that ease is part of the genetics of what he partly comes out of. And yet all of his values are bourgeois. All of his values are middling and mercantile. All of his values are this society's as it now is.

Would Douglas-Home have joined or even given money to United Against Fascism, who he would have regarded as smelly little people on the margins of society who were a Left-wing rabble who probably need to be beating the grass somewhere? Or in my regiment. You see what I mean? The idea that he would identify with these people because the real enemy represents the seeds of the aristocracy from which one has fled, that wouldn't occur to him. He was too much what he was, basically, as a form to really consider these lies and this legerdemain and this flight of fancy.

One comes to the most controversial area of Evola's entire prognosis, and this is the belief that Jewishness is responsible for decline and that they are a distinct and another race that pushes upon things and causes things to fall and be destroyed. These are the views, of course, the belief that there is a morphic element in the nature of the decline, that has made him so untouchable and controversial. The interesting thing is when he was approached about *The Protocols of the Elders of Zion*, which is believed by all liberal humanist scholars to be a forgery of the Okhrana secret police based upon an alleged French novel, I think in the nineteenth century, Evola said, "I'm not concerned whether it's a forgery or not," which is a very interesting response.

Because in Evola's occultistic and Hermetic view of the world, you can indicate something through its reversal, you can indicate something through metaphorization, something can be emotionally true and not completely factually true, a text can be used to exemplify truths deeper than its own surface. This is a religious view of the text, of course, that the text does not end with itself. It's a Medieval view and is based upon a science of linguistic study called hermeneutics where you would look at every word, you would look at every paragraph, you would look at every piece of syntax to deconstruct for essence rather than deconstruct to find the absence of essence.

In the Western world, if you go to university now and you do any humanities, any arts, any liberal arts, or any social science course, you will come across an ideology called deconstruction. Even vaguely, the semi-educated have heard of it. This is a viewpoint that says that any essentialisms (race, class isn't an essentialism, but it begins to become one in the minds of man, belief in God, gender, and so on) lead to the gates of Auschwitz. This is what deconstruction is based on as a theory. Therefore you look at every text, you look at every film, because they're obsessed with mass culture, you see, looking at what the masses look at and what they're fed by the capitalist cultural machine. And they look at this and they say, "Oh look, dangerous essentialism there. Did you see that, in that John Wayne film? Did you see the way he spoke to the Red Indian? Sorry, Native American." You see, that sort of thing. You look at these things and you break them down and you break them down again and you break down the element of sort of "David Duke" logic that could be said to lie in that particular phrasing and so on.

But the sort of analysis that Evola maintains is what you might call constructionism rather than deconstructionism. And that's building upon the essences of things and bringing out their discriminatory differences. So to him, the fact that that text may have been put into circulation by the Okhrana, the Czarist secret police, as a profound Hermetic, metaphoricization for courses of history which may or may not be occurring, is worthy of study. He again returns to the idea that everything has meaning.

If you want war with the Islamic world, the towers will fall. If you want a pacifist and isolationist America to enter the

Great War, a particular boat with civilians onboard but weapons underneath, will be torpedoed by the Germans. If you
want to get the isolationist boobs of middle America into a
global struggle in the early 1940s, you allow the prospect of an
attack that you know is going to happen to occur. And you
make sure that your aircraft carriers are not there. And you
blame the middling officers who were there for their incompe-
tence retrospectively. Because it is the moment to kick-start
democratic engagement with heroic and Spartan activities.

Who can doubt that there is a streak of the Spartan, when an
American Marine goes up a beach on Iwo Jima or when he
fights in Fallujah? Some of the modern world has certainly fall-
en away for that man as he faces oblivion in warriorship
against the Other, even within the modern. And people like
Evola and Jünger would realize that. There's even at times, in
the extremity of modern warfare, a return to the individual.
What about these American pilots and these other pilots, these
Russian pilots, who fly in these planes, and the warrior is part
of the plane? You know, they have a computer in their visor
and they have all sorts of statistics that are coming up before
them. And it's like a man who's an army fighting on his own,
isn't it? He's got an amount of force under his wings which is
equivalent to an army of centuries ago. So, you have a return to
elite individuals trained only for killing and warriorship at the
top tier of present Western advanced military metaphysics.

Because the interesting thing about Evola's way of thinking
is it's creative. Most Right-wing people are pessimistic intro-
verts who don't like the world they were born into, but Evola
seems to me to be in some ways an extravagant, optimistic aristocrat who always sees, not the best side of everything, but the
most heroic side of everything that goes beyond even itself.
Even if *The Protocols of the Elders of Zion*, in accordance with his
diction, was a lie and can be proved to be such, the fact that
millions were motivated to believe in it, millions to reject its
causation, that people fought out the consequences, and the
consequences of the consequences, in relation to even some of
those ideas, means that it is of great specificity and import.

Nietzsche has the idea that a man stands on the edge of a

pond, and he skims a pebble into the pond, and it skips across the water. You know, when you get it skimming right and it goes and it goes and it goes, and wave upon wave moves upon the surface, and you can't predict the formulation of the wave and the current that it leads into. And that history has unknown consequences.

The Maoist general who was asked by an American sympathizer after the Maoist Long March, itself partly mythological, "What's your view of the French Revolution?" And he memorably replied, "It's too early to tell." Because it's only two hundred years back. That is the sort of perspective that Evola has.

And although there will be crushing defeats, and men are now of his sort, aristocrats, for whom the modern world has no time, play polo, waste your money, go to brothels, gamble all the time. There's no role for you. The world is ruled by machines and money and committees and Barack Obama.

You know, American Rightists call Obama "Obamination" instead of abomination. It's like a bit in a Marvel comic, actually, but never mind. Isn't he the signification for everything that is declining in America? And aren't all of these middle-class tax revolt-type movements, which are one hundred percent, what should we call them, grassroots American, aren't they really within the allowed channels of opposition? "He's a socialist!" "It's all about tax. It's not about anything else." "It's all within the remit of health care budgetary constraints and views on same." Etcetera, etcetera. "What about the deficit?" Aren't all of these movements and the sort of rage that they contain elements and spectrums of what he would call anti-modernity, or semi-anti-modernity within modernity?

None of us know what the future will hold, but it is quite clear that unless people of advanced type in our group believe in some of the traditions that they come out of again, they will disappear. And in Evola's view, they will deserve to disappear. So, my view is that whatever one's view, whatever one's system of faith . . . and don't forget in the Greek world, you could disbelieve in the gods and think they were metaphors, you could kneel before a statue of them, or you could have a philosophical belief in between the two, and all were part of the same culture, all were part of the same city-state, and if called upon as free citizens to defend it, even Socrates would stand in line with his shield and his spear.

All of Evola's books are now available on the Internet. The most controversial passages about morphology and ethnicity are all available on the Internet. Read Julius Evola. Read an aristocrat for the past and the future, and look back at the perennial Traditions that are part and parcel of Western civilization and can fuel the imagination and fire even in those who don't entirely believe in them.

Thank you very much!

Yukio Mishima[*]

Mishima's life was dedicated to a return of the spirit of the samurai and a belief in Yamamoto Jōchō's book *Hagakure*, which is partly the seventeenth-century bible of samurai morality whereby life is transfigured by death, and the notion of a warrior who's also an intellectual and literary figure as well as a spiritual crusader, a priest who kills, is paramount.

Japanese culture is distinct from almost all others on Earth and is still difficult to understand and conceptualize for many Westerners. One of the more glaring things about Japan is that material which is banned in the West is widely available, particularly in terms of pornography, over which there are very little restrictions at all. Even in manga, or Japanese comics, which are often amazingly hardline and hardcore in Western terms.

Japan is a strange society, because the dialectics that move within it are oppositional and highly differentiated to those of the West. It's probably true that people who are self-identifying in the Western tradition have often admired elements about Japan, particularly Imperial Japan. There's a degree to which there's not so much a symmetry as a meaningful asymmetry by which the Japanese are perceived as a people who wanted to be themselves in their own way.

Japanese thought is influenced by Confucian, Shintoist, Buddhist, Zen Buddhist, and Taoist ideas, and a medley of these finds itself in the basis of what it is to be Japanese. One of the cardinal views is that life is dominated by the spirits of ancestors, and there's the notion of ancestor worship, which makes the family and the line of a family's inheritance extraordinarily important. These spirits are called *kami*, and there's the notion that they can intervene in one's actual life. These are supernatural ideas, but one of the tricks of Japanese culture,

---

[*] This lecture was originally delivered to the English New Right in London on December 10, 2011. The transcript was made by V. S.

which is very similar to ancient Greece in this respect, is that all orders of opinion can accept these beliefs because there are secular and atheistic interpretations of these belief systems as there are purely religious ones. As in ancient Greece, a woman could kneel or lie before a statue of a god, and yet rationalist intellectuals in the same civilization could regard the divine stories as entirely metaphorical. And yet they would all be accepted as Greek, and they would all be accepted as different definitions of what it was to be Greek or to be a member of a Greek city-state. Mishima, for one, was obsessed by Greece, particularly ancient Greece, and incorporated quite a few Grecian odes and ethics into his books.

Mishima was born into an upper middle-class family in Tokyo and was separated from his other siblings by his grandmother at an early age. A weak and rather effeminate child who was divorced from the company of boys on the orders of his grandmother, who was obsessed with death and had a rather morbid outlook and was herself quite closely related to key members of the Japanese aristocracy. Mishima had a strange, rather twilight childhood up to the age of 12, when his grandmother died and he was reintroduced starkly to the rest of his family.

Modern and somewhat psychoanalytical interpretations of Mishima's later conduct and ritual suicide as a political gesture at the end of his life concentrate on these early years as the foundation stones of the cult of living death that his adoration of the samurai was to perpetuate.

Now, Mishima started writing when he was about 12 years of age, possibly when he was 6 years of age, and had his first novel produced when he was between 16 and 18, which was published on war ration paper. The first book was called *Confessions of a Mask*, but there was a book even before that which is largely forgotten today and which concerns nature worship.

Mishima wrote a wide number of books. He wrote plays, which are both modern and classical in the Japanese tradition. Noh theater, as it's called, Kabuki theater is a classical tradition in Japan, and there's also a puppet theater in relation to the second city other than Tokyo, Osaka, and the provinces. The tradition being external to Tokyo, the puppet is used instead of the body. In Tokyo, the body is used instead of a puppet. He also wrote two modern plays, one of which was called *Madame de Sade*, which is about the Marquis de Sade's long-suffering wife in the early years of their life. That's Donatien Alphonse François de Sade, who lived between 1740 and 1814. And he also wrote a play called *My Friend Hitler*, which is quite controversial and was published in English, I think, in 1966.

His most famous work, which is widely regarded outside Japan, is a tetralogy at the end of his life called *The Sea of Fertility* and which is about the increasing meaninglessness of Japanese civilization, as he saw it, dominated by an excess of materialism which was alien to it.

Japan began to modernize from what Westerners would call a feudal type of life or pattern of existence in the 1860s and underwent extraordinary modernization. So much so that it is the first hybridized, Westernized Eastern society, or Occidentally-oriented Asiatic society, seen in Western terms. I say "seen in Western terms," because Westerners can only ever see things in their own terms. It's extraordinarily difficult to step out of one's own culture and view another culture which is highly advanced and technocratically proficient as well as having an artistry that stretches back centuries, if not a thousand years plus, into the past and yet is based upon axioms which are fundamentally different to one's own.

To give one example, there is a species of violent comic book, manga as they're called in Japan, which is extremely sadistic and erotic, and one of these publications is called *Rape-man*, rather like Spider-Man or Superman, and it's aimed at a similar audience. The incidence of rape in Japan is extraordinarily small in comparison to other advanced meritocratic and post-industrial societies like the United States, because the Japanese view is that you exteriorize dangerous fantasies by demarcating their existence rather than repressing them. The idea being that life is so ordered and structured in accordance with the social organicism of Japan based upon Confucian ideals that you have to let off some steam from the pressure-cooker eventually, and one of the ways to do this is with material that will be regarded as suggestive, extremist, anti-familial, or highly dangerous in Western terms. So, you have a culture of extreme restraint and the possibility of radical violence coexisting in the same continuum, because a lot of Japanese ethics and super-abundant ethics, the meta-ethics of a society, are about the holding together of contraries in a dynamic state of force.

Much of the Western world became aware of the growing militancy of the Japanese Imperial nation-state in and around the beginning of the twentieth century, when Japan fought the first successful war against a European or a Western society when they essentially defeated the Russian Empire. This was in the Russo-Japanese War, which led to the scenario of a European power (Russia would be regarded as a greater European power in these circumstances, its landmass stretching over into Asia) defeated by a non-Occidental rival. This was the first intimation of the modern prowess of Japan, that it was prepared to take on major Occidental societies in the struggle for world hegemony.

The doctrines that have ruled Japan are essentially those of Imperial monarchy, but this was always vitiated by the idea of the Shogun, or Shogunate, whereby essentially militaristic feudal lords representing samurai clans drawn from different parts of Japan exercised the Imperial advisory role underneath a monarchical overlay. The monarch was seen as appointed by God and were seen as divine. It's important to understand that for most Japanese until the middle of the twentieth century, following the defeat, the divinity of the Emperor was sacrosanct and was not negotiable and was not subject to discussion.

In extreme Right circles in Japan, one of the many reasons why Mishima is a controversial figure is because he's criticized the Emperor Hirohito at the end of the Second World War, when in fact he didn't abdicate and agreed to the American proposals that the Japanese constitution be fundamentally changed.

It's difficult to imagine a human being who's worshipped as a god in Western terms. Roman emperors were worshipped as gods, but only outside Italy proper and only often in the more backward and remote parts of the Empire. Even totalitarian leaders of Western nations in the twentieth century who developed around them an anima or an aura which could be said to be spiritistic in type have never been worshipped as gods in the formal sense.

The de-divinization of the leadership of Japan in the postwar period was part of the American recasting of Japan so that it would never be a threat again. Japan has one of the largest standing armies in accordance with its population in the world, and all it does is guard the territory of Japan and steam around the various islands that constitute that landmass. There's a degree to which the Japanese Self-Defense Force, as it's called, never intervenes in the rest of the world, and you will notice that, UN proscriptions aside, America has not been able to coax Japan out into the various escapades and forms of adventurism which have characterized both the Cold War and the immediate last twenty years after the destabilization of the Soviet Union and the emergence of the Russian Federation in its stead. Japan takes no role even in the Vietnam War. The Americans would have loved Japan to have fought in the Vietnam War, because of close proximity, but they refused to do so.

There's a strong culture of civic pacifism in Japan rooted in the nihilistic despair and vaporization of the atomic weapons that we used. There's even a form of revisionism in Japan which is partly state-induced and which is not compatible with other forms of historical revisionism elsewhere in the world. This is the idea that certain official sources and channels and mainstream media in Japan downplay the actual sort of ferocious and horrific events of the atomic weapons use, because they don't want to draw attention to the war of annihilation struggle and Imperial dominion and the desire to carve out an enormous socioeconomic empire in near Asia that Japan was engaged in. This means that the victims of the bombing, and there were an enormous number of survivors in both of the cities, blame their own government for perpetuating the war against the United States and its Western allies and in alliance with Nazi Germany and Fascist Italy. This is a Western ideology which has been seized upon by the victims of the atomic strikes and is often very powerfully used inside Japan. So, you have this paradoxical idea that revisionism is state playing-down of Hiroshima and Nagasaki so as to defeat the neo-pacifism of a largely Buddhist movement that seeks to hold the Japanese government as being co-responsible for the use of the atomic weapons, when in actual fact in all logic the Americans used the atomic weapons. This is part of a device that is used in Japan to regulate and moderate anti-Americanism, which is still a latent and powerful force in Japanese society given the re-writing of the constitution and the creation of a new civic Japan after the war.

Basically, Japan was changed by the advent of the Second World War and its nuclear-laced aftermath far more than Germany was in the period of Adenauer's succession between 1945 and 1948. West Germany largely was built on the basis, somewhat rudimentarily, of Weimar Germany, which could be said to be its natural precursor. There's also a degree to which the norms of West Germany and its domination by the Christian Democratic and Social Democratic power structure, alternating with periodic elections and with a federal system based initially in Bonn prior to reunification, was such that it ramified with many of the states around Germany in Europe. Japan had to chart a totally new course after the Second World War.

You'll notice that Japan is dominated, or has been until relatively recently, by one political party. Despite numerous elections, despite numerous attempts to import the Western model into Japan, two-party democracy has never really taken off.

One party, somewhat meaninglessly called the Liberal Democratic Party to appease American sort of neo-imperial tastes, has dominated the country since the nuclear explosions and the de-divinization of the Emperor and the resulting capitulation of the armed forces, most of which did not commit ritual suicide on the event of Japan's defeat because the Emperor ordered them to stand down.

Mishima represents the culture of the Imperial officer corps who fought the war in Imperial Japanese stead, against first China and then against the Western powers. It's important to recognize that Japan initially thought about attacking the Soviet Union—Russia, in a sense—rather than the United States. This is partly because Japan had fought a war successfully against Russia in the early part of the twentieth century, but it's also because a significantly Right-wing part of the samurai-based officer corps wanted to attack the underbelly of the Soviet Union. Don't forget, we have a situation in the 1930s where large sections of China are occupied by Japan, particularly the industrial area of Manchuria. There was also in Western and humanist terms extreme brigandage and ferocity and what is called atrocity in those areas committed by Japanese troops.

If Japan had invaded the Soviet Union's softer underbelly and gone up into the Asiatic republics of what was then the Soviet Union at the time of maximum tension in the Soviet Union and during a period where the Soviet Union was under extreme attack, at the point of near-defeat, by the forces of Nazi Germany, the Soviet Union possibly could have been defeated and destroyed, and the whole history of the world would have been different. Indeed, in 1934 or 1936, there was a rising by four thousand officers, all of whom were accredited samurai, which took over Tokyo and which demanded that the Imperial general staff orient Japan's would-be offensive effort against the Soviet Union, both for patriotic, geopolitical, and historical reasons. Also because Communism was seen as a great threat to the Imperialistic and dynastic system that ruled in Japan.

The samurai are a type of soldierly elite that has existed in other cultures in the world, but rarely has been concretized to the degree that took place in Japan. At times in Japanese history, ten percent of the population were accredited samurai, including women who were married into samurai clans. The samurai were meant to be learned warriors who were steeped in the Buddhist tradition, which is in some ways, in Western terms, a mildly pacifist tradition, but the hard edge of the tradition is the martial arts, which the samurai learn in their initial training.

Samurais are accredited, unless they're independent of all lords, to a lord or to a feudal baron in Western terms, and they formed clans or inter-ethnic enclaves or forms of identity which identified with particular feudal lords as against others.

You then built up into a Shogunate whereby an Imperial leader and his wife or wives, because most marriages at the upper end of Japanese society were arranged . . . You had relationships with wives, you had possible relationships with geishas of which there were different types, and you had the possibility of multiple wives and multiple families for some members of the Japanese ruling class and upper class.

One important thing to remember about Japan is that Japan is a society that rejected Christianity formerly and in an extreme way. There is a degree to which few societies on Earth have partly begun a conversion to Christianity and then reversed and negated it involving the massacre of many Christians and Christian missionaries. Exposed to the Portuguese and the Spanish empires, Japan hesitated over the adoption of Christianity, and whole samurai clans in various parts of Japan converted to the Christian faith. This was later undone by later Shogunates who returned to Shintoism, or to innate Japanese paganism.

This faith system believes that the Japanese are uniquely chosen on Earth and are the children of the Sun and are represented governmentally and institutionally and metaphysically by a living Sun god who is their Emperor.

The duty of the samurai is to kill with love and understanding, and in accordance with complete serenity in a semi-religious way on behalf of this divine autocrat or leader, even if his will is interpreted by a Bismarckian figure such as a Shogun. Again, one strives for Western metaphors to understand elements of the Japanese mindset, because it is rare for this formulation to exist in Western culture.

Simulacrums of the samurai in the Western tradition might be said to be the Templars and the Hospitalers in the Middle Ages, or elitist Christian warriors reared to a patriarchal standard of ascetic masculinity, those who believed ideologically in Crusades against Islam, for example, on behalf of the faith and genuinely seemed to believe in them at the time when they professed those views. One also possibly has elites in all armies, such as the Praetorian elite in the Roman legions, the Spartan courage and system of land-based fighting, the corollary to the Athenian naval-based military prowess which provided the balance in Greek military warfare that enabled them to resist Persian invasion and elsewhere. But the cultivation of a priesthood that is also a killing machine, which is what the samurai were, is difficult to understand in Western terms.

In the *Hagakure*, the samurai must never show weakness even at a point of weakness, and must never speak in a way that undermines his sense of self or his loyalty to his lord and master. Samurai should strive for this odd combination of fanaticism, steeliness, clearness of thought, and serenity of temper. The samurai should feel no guilt over killing, but the flip side of this is that the samurai is always ready to kill himself in relation to a system of honor.

In the Japanese traditionalist belief system, suicide is morally meritorious, which is something that the Western mind finds difficult to comprehend. This is because Shintoism preaches the notion of direct reincarnation as a fact rather than just as an idea that can be spiritually postulated. In samurai rhetoric and law, and these ideas have the force of law for this pre-existent military elite inside Japan, if you were killed or if you committed ritual suicide, you were immediately reborn in a mother's womb forty days later as a new human being. This meant that in their conception of self, suicide was not the end. Most of the greatest and most glorious figures in Japanese culture have committed suicide and have been praised for this, both in their own time and afterwards. All suicides have to write a poem before they die which is called a death poem, and is often in the form of a haiku, this minimalist, condensed type of poetry, often dealing with themes of gentleness and forgiveness prior to the ultimate form of death.

Mishima believed that this is what Japan was and is and could be, and he believed that the spirit of the samurai, both male and female, fluctuated in Japan and should be brought back in a period where it had been relaxed to a point of semi-oblivion in the late 1940s, 1950s, 1960s, and up to his own *seppuku* in 1970, when he ended his own life on the 25th of November 1970 in a way which caused consternation.

There is no parallel in the West for this sort of thing. If you like, the most prominent post-war British Western novelist is somebody called William Golding, who wrote *The Lord of the Flies*. It's like William Golding committing suicide on the steps of Downing Street after having demanded a change of course by a post-war British prime minister drawn from either the Labour or Conservative tradition, and also having spent his entire life getting physically fit to a point of military perfection rather than being a sort of flabby *Guardian* aesthete, which essentially he was.

It's also redolent of a man who owned his own private army, which Mishima developed for his own use. This was a society called the Shield Society, and consisted of military trainees and conscripts about a hundred in number that were run as a quasi-paramilitary force by Mishima and were allowed to train in Japanese army camps after 1966. Mishima's ritual suicide took place in an army camp in 1970.

The liberal Western interpretation of Mishima's life is a failed attempt to return to the samurai verities of old, which remains concurrent with the literary output that is highly revered in the West and outside Japan. Westerners as well as Easterners put Mishima forward for three Nobel Prize citations in the post-war period, yet he never won, partly because another Japanese writer who was very much his literary sponsor won the prize in 1968, and Japanese culture is so difficult to understand from many mainstream Western perspectives that it was felt that in that generational era, another Japanese wouldn't win the prize after it had been adopted to one of their own number. So, Mishima became gradually aware of the fact that he would have to wait for that. It's widely believed that he deserved the prize, as a number of other major writers in the Western world have done, but have not received it.

Mishima's literary output is divided into two halves, one of which deals with, if you like, quite decadent themes in certain respects. Mishima is drawn to extremes, and in *Confessions of a Mask* he's drawn to extremes of auto-mutilation and sacrifice of self and the wearing of masks as part of social identity. The concept of the mask is cardinal to what it is to be Japanese. So frightened are the Japanese of giving offense which will lead to extreme violence between individuals and/or between groups, that a culture of extremely formal politeness is institutionalized whereby no one wants to be seen to lose face in relation to a rival, a family member, a competitor, or somebody they're associated with in business, commerce, or state practice. This is quite opposed to the post-1960s belief in the Western world of emotional authentication, whereby people are professed to express their emotions, particularly in public. Otherwise they will be belaboring under false consciousness or will be internally divided or troubled. In Jungian psychoanalysis or analytical psychology, there is the belief that all people have a shadow which is their more negative, ferocious, adversarial, and barbaric side, and to be a whole human being, this has to be integrated into the personality. In the Japanese way of thinking, this is already integrated into the personality and doesn't need to be shown, because it would lead to conflict of a very barbaric manner.

There's an extreme tension in Japanese society, and there are strong sadomasochistic features from a Western viewpoint in a society that holds itself taut and rigid, almost like a man in archery who's just about to release a longbow. And yet at the same time, there is a softness and a gentility and an aesthetic decorum, especially about traditional Japanese attitudes, which strikes a Westerner as a belief in perfection and stylization. This ability to slip from stylization—the tea ceremony, for example, which is a key samurai ritual copied by the rest of the culture and which has to be separated from just tea drinking in an English sort of 4:30 in the afternoon way—and the possibility of extreme violence, which is always the legacy of the samurai tradition, and which lies at the heart of a lot of Japanese notions of themselves.

The culture of the manga or the film on paper which is the comic book, which in the West is essentially regarded as a form for children and adolescents which has to be outgrown when one transfers to proper books, and the adult version of which is the film, rather than the comic or graphic novel. In Japan, some of the most senior artists and senior political figures in the society are people who write comic books, which are regarded as a major cultural form and are sold in their millions, if not their tens of millions.

An enormous subculture within manga, which deals with every topic on Earth from cooking to romance to war worship, is the samurai genre, which spills over into television, film, and books. Many of the samurai novels and plays and films strike Western audiences as stereotypical, but a Western parallel would be the fantasy of the western in the United States. Everyone has probably seen *A Fistful of Dollars* with Clint Eastwood and has seen *The Magnificent Seven* and these sorts of westerns, all of which are based upon Japanese samurai films and cultural abstracts of that sort.

One of the most remarkable samurai films of all time is by the greatest Japanese director, as many conceive it inside and outside Japan since the Second World War, a man called Kurosawa who did a film called *Ran*, which means "chaos" and which is the samurai version of *King Lear*, which with *Hamlet* is Shakespeare's preeminent play, possibly next to *Macbeth, Othello*, and many others. This Japanese *King Lear*, which is an extraordinary piece of work and lasts for about four hours, is an attempt to distill the samurai ethic using a Western story. This is still controversial in Japan. Although many Japanese artists have been famous outside Japan, the belief in cultural and ethnic exclusivity is very extreme in Japan by Western standards even to this day.

Kurosawa was heavily criticized for using a Western model in order to transmute Japanese meaning and form. It is still controversial even to use extra-Japanese cultural forms in classical Japanese usage, even within modernity.

Mishima got around this partly by transmuting Japanese forms in ways that Westerners could understand. In his novel called *The Temple of the Golden Pavilion*, he deals with a burning down of a Buddhist shrine by a psychopathic eccentric who was a classical outsider in terms that both Western and Eastern audiences could understand but not necessarily sympathize with. The book caused consternation in Japan and was based on a true case. The nearest parallel I can think of is Truman Capote's non-fiction novel *In Cold Blood*, which is about the murder of a Kansas family by two mid-American drifters whose internal psychological torments and anxieties are dealt with at extreme length by Capote prior to their judicial killing by the federal American system in, I think, an Iowa penitentiary in the late 1960s.

Mishima believed that a culture should be exclusive and that Japanese life and circumstances were unique and demanded unique answers inside Japan which were purely Japanese. Like all artists, his form of nationalism was one which did not necessarily appeal to Right-wing nationalists inside Japan.

Paul Schrader's film, which is a very famous Hollywood film, and for a Hollywood film it's a very good film, called *Mishima: A Life in Four Chapters* . . . Schrader's most famous for his extremely violent, excoriating film about the transgression of American values called *Taxi Driver*, a film which many people will have seen or at least heard of. Now, in his film about Mishima, three of Mishima's novels, one from *The Sea of Fertility* tetralogy, are reconfigured as stories external to Mishima's life, but which he gives literary value to by virtue of his own biography. The fourth quadrant of the film is biographical/autobiographical and deals with Mishima's own life.

Now, in Schrader's piece, Mishima is seen as a man whose death is foretold by the nature of the ideology he adopts. One which is both an emotional, a literary, a speculative, a martial, and an intellectual ideology. The sort of ideology that Mishima proposed in his novels and plays was similar to that put forward by D. H. Lawrence in the West, and yet different, with similar elements to Friedrich Nietzsche's thought at the end of the nineteenth century, and yet distinct.

There was something also irreducibly "other" and Japanese about it which no Westerner could completely grasp. I think there is something in the Western tradition, which although not frightened of suicide, regards it with a degree of disrespect. Certainly the idea that a suicide can be beautiful and is the apotheosis of a life and of a moment of religious intensity is not alien to the West, but it is relatively alien to the West and has attracted few ideological adherents in most forms of Western history.

The main Western group that preaches suicide at the moment is the Italian-American Sicilian Mafia, whereby a Mafia don who is cornered by his colleagues and has nowhere to go is meant to open his veins in a warm bath, as certain senators and other leaders of the Roman Republic and Empire did in the ancient world. But the Western view of warriorship is always to try and survive so that you can fight on. Western terrorists rarely ever kill themselves, no matter how violent or fixated or paramilitary the logic of their own language and being might be. IRA men, UDA men, whatever they might have been, would inflict pain and violence but always seek to get away afterwards, and this is very much the Western ethic in battle. The idea of a deliberate sacrifice of self, which will occur in slaughter anyway, because soldierly rearing and military training is partly being trained for death, as all people in military command structures understand, because military life is where emotions are heightened to a degree which civilian life can no longer cope with the exertions, particularly the moral exertions which are required.

The nearest Western version to a man like Mishima, who in a way superseded him because he had a military background that Mishima couldn't boast, and because of the feebleness of Mishima's body when he came to be commissioned in the Japanese Imperial Army at the Second World War couldn't ascribe to, is Ernst Jünger. Ernst Jünger is probably the supreme example of an artist, a literati, a secular spiritualist, and an extreme soldier who fought in the First World War for four years from 1914 to 1918, was awarded two Iron Crosses as well as the highest medal for valor, the *Pour le Mérite* of the Prussian Imperial Army, and was wounded fourteen times at the front to which he returned and only stood down with the surrender of the German Imperial forces at the armistice at the end of that conflict in 1918. If you read books like *Fire and Blood*, which is only available in German, or *Battle as Inner Experience*, which is likewise only available in German, or the two versions of his four-pronged wartime epic, which are available in English, *The Storm of Steel* and *Copse 125*, you come across a man who has a spiritual view of warfare and could be described as a Western samurai.

The samurai tradition basically believes that the potential of a soldier has to be high rather than low. It's the combination of a university professor, a martial arts bodybuilder, and an extreme warrior. And this is an unusual combination which in most societies has only been restricted to tiny little militaristic elites, or elites that guard an imperial or quasi-divine figure. The Praetorian Guards, the Immortals in the Persian court, an organization that was partly reinvigorated by the Shah of Iran during his period of power, the SS to a degree, and similar organizations that would now be called special forces are the nearest you get in the Western tradition to the samurai ethic. But even then, your average SAS man could hardly be described as an intellectual or a literati. Nor is that insisted upon. However, the degree of physical courage, hardness, rectitude, and readiness for martial conflict which Delta Force, the Navy SEALs in the United States, the Spetsnaz forces in the post-Soviet Russia, the Special Air Service Regiment and Special Boat Service Regiment and the elite squads of the German and Italian army, and probably the elite of the French Foreign Legion as well could be said to carry out and do carry out in Western neo-imperial missions all over the Third World to this day are the nearest you get to the sort of endless military training and subservience to authority that the samurai had to evince.

There's also the combination of a degree of individualism as well, because these are warriors who are bound to have to fight on their own, often behind enemy lines, and it's noticeable in the enormous literature which prevails in modern Britain, or post-modern Britain, of the SAS warrior, the Andy McNab subcultures and all their endless spin-offs and various media whereby SAS men and their equivalents are sort of worshipped because of the yearning for a heroic figure and the yearning of a return to elements of heroic masculinity which are shot through with individuality. But again, despite all the courage and military preponderance that such individual warriors, and individualistic warriors at that, will show, there is not the culture of a refined ethic of beauty, the religious sensibility, or the cult of intellectuality, which although a small minority of sam-

urai would actually have evinced in their own era was nevertheless the guiding ideology of this type. The combination of
the warrior and the aesthete is not uniquely Japanese, but the
ideology that pushed them together was, and to a certain extent still is.

After Japan modernized its society in the 1860s, the Japanese
Imperial ruling class went for a national conscript army along
Western lines, but the whole officer corps and the whole elite of
the Japanese army after the defeat of the Shogunate, which involved a monarchical restoration in conceptual terms after the
1860s, was samurai in order and orientation. This in turn gets
us into a very controversial area which most studies of Mishima, which tend to be purely literary in form, tend to reject. This
is the treatment of Western prisoners by the Japanese Imperial
Army during the Second World War.

Many Westerners still remember hideous disfigurements,
malnutrition, and mistreatment of prisoners, both Western and
Eastern, by the Imperial Japanese Army. The Mishimas of this
world never really commented on this because their system of
moral ethics in this is in some ways different to a dualist, a
Manichaean, or a Christian or Christianized, or post-Christian
system. In Mishima's conception of the world, without speaking for him unduly, although it's there in texts such as *The Way
of the Samurai* and *Sun and Steel* and "the pathway of the samurai is death," and books about the heroic martyrs of the Japanese Imperial Army, is that pain and cruelty are part of life and
are on a continuum with peace and benignity, so there's a degree to which there is not a moral soul-searching about what is
regarded as evil in other spiritual trajectories, although there
would be no denial that evil can exist and that men in battle
will perpetuate it.

The important thing about the sort of pagan morality that
the samurai evinced is that it was hierarchical rather than dual.
Rather than behaving well or badly, a society such as this or a
caste such as this drawn from a society, which it probably was
quite unrepresentative of, as such elites always are, has a hierarchical notion of morality whereby honor and the esteem that
one is held in by one's warrior colleagues is more important

than dualist preparations. So, a samurai who has disobeyed an order or who's been caught in a cowardly act or has retreated before the enemy will be demanded to commit ritual suicide instantly. Instantly! Just like that, with little preparation. Just has to be mentally prepared for this. Traditionally, samurai would cut the tops of their fingers off for minor indiscretions and for minor infractions of various rules in their honor-based system, which is called *bushido*. And there is a sort of cultivation of the masochism of the flesh as well as the extremity of externalized violence, which is a Japanese tradition and which essentially affects their attitudes in all areas: aesthetic, literary, poetic, religious, and sensual and sexual as well. So, Japanese culture contains some very extreme metaphysical postulates which are openly avowed, in a sense, whereas in most societies such tendencies are often hidden or glossed over or regarded with a certain degree of discretion.

The radicalism of the Japanese army during its expansionist phase and its ferocity towards enemies, as well as its deep sense of discipline and self-control, was commented upon by many people at the time. Indeed, in the Rape of Nanking, for example, the German ambassador in a society which Germany at that time was then moving towards alignment with, West and East, described the conduct of Japanese troops as bestial, viewed in traditional Western terms. And this was a German cultural attaché at that particular Chinese embassy which had been invaded from without by the Japanese Imperial Army.

There's a degree to which Mishima, like Jünger about the excesses that the Prussian tradition can go in for on occasion, remains silent about these sorts of matters, much to the extreme anger of humanistic and moral Western critics. This is because their view of life is aesthetically different and supercharged in relation to what is currently part of present civility.

One of Mishima's remarks about his own civilization was its feminization, which was something that a large number of culturally Right-wing criticizers of their own societies have put forward in the post-war period. It is quite true that the army and the military tradition has completely vacated the civilized and the civic space in nearly all Western societies, including the

United States. Armies are purely professional and are no longer conscript. The bulk of the population never comes anywhere
near armed force or the utilization of that force. Young Westernized men never go in for military training. One of the last
Western countries to get rid of military training for the young
was France. Always done on the lines of cost and because the
military don't want a large number of the conscripts that they
regard as very substandard troops that they have to lick into
shape for sociological reasons, and wouldn't be much good
martially. This is why you have a confluence of cost-cutting,
neo-liberal politicians, and army and navy and air force tech-
nocrats who wish to get rid of conscript armies. Interestingly,
in France's case, the last two political parties that voted for the
tradition of mass military conscription were the Front National
and the Communist Party of France. All of the parties in between them, in the middle if you like, center-Left and center-
Right, voted for a paid, patriotic army of volunteers who were
not going to interfere with the business of military life.

It's always true, of course, that armies constellate around
elites, and even a professional vanguard army of people who
wish to fight in such a force on behalf of their own nation-state
or confederation form an elite in relation to the mass of the citizenry, but never before has the citizenry been so disempow-
ered in relation to military life.

Mishima didn't preach the militarization of Japanese life,
which is what somebody like Ernst Jünger preached for inter-
war Germany in the 1920s and 1930s. There is a degree to
which Mishima's belief was that the army should once again
become the template of Japanese civilian life and should become the model for a post-war Japan which related to the pre-
war Japan that went down in atomic defeat.

After writing the better part of a hundred novels and plays
and non-fiction works, at least forty of which stand alone as
literary items — the West will quickly run off items for money
— Mishima proposed a solution to the dilemma of post-war
Japan. Japan has been politically crucified in certain respects
since the Second [World] War, as has Germany. A very powerful country economically, and yet a country with almost no

military resource outside or external to its own borders, and a country where people are afraid to summon up any foreign policy that can conflict with American global prerequisites.

There's a degree to which the Japan of the post-war era is a politically humiliated society and a militarily humiliated society which is also an economic superpower. Germany, certainly in relation to the rest of the European Union, is in much the same situation. Both countries have internalized their massive defeats in the second global conflagration of the twentieth century. Both have related to those defeats in different ways. Both have engaged in an endless politics of apology and absence of self-defense in relation to what hostile Western historians tend to call the unmastered past.

Don't forget, although it's regarded as obscure by most Westerners, the entire Japanese military leadership, often in a symbolic way, was put on trial after the Second World War. Massive war crimes trials were conducted along the Nuremberg patent despite the fact that atomic weapons had been used in order to finish the conflict on the Japanese peninsula. The Japanese elite has internalized the idea that the use of the atomic weapons was justified because of the possible several million deaths that would have accrued when samurai-based warriors on the Japanese mainland fighting for a god-king, as they perceived the Empire cult at that time, would have wreaked havoc and would have killed an enormous number of Americans and other Western allies and paid the price in terms of body count themselves. In this way of looking at things or point of reference, the Western historiographical tradition regards the use of the atomic weapons, the only time they've ever been used in anger by one nation-state against another, as justified, partly because it saved so much chaos and rancor which would have been occasioned by a conventional invasion of Japan. Although there is deep anger in Japan about the use of these weapons, in typical fashion, a lot of that anger has been turned inwards inside Japanese culture in relation to pacifist usage, possible feminization of life seen in masculine, traditional samurai, and martial terms, and in terms of the Buddhist tradition.

There's little social anger towards the United States in a

publically affordable way, and this is because the United States has completely dominated and morally and mentally invaded post-war Japan to a degree that most Westerners cannot configure. It's only because Japanese culture is so distinct and free-standing and resistant to Westernization in some of its own terms that Westerners don't realize how much post-war Japan has been Westernized in America's image.

Now, the belief that one author, rather like Ezra Pound in relation to Fascist Italy as regards the governmental structures and economic power of the United States, could change this is part of the fantasy of what it is to be an important literary writer, particularly one who believes in the bardic tradition. The idea that writers speak for a whole people or writers speak for something more important than themselves. The liberal conception of the writer is of essentially a lonely creature scribbling or tapping away on a computer now in a room whose products are sold and bought as any other commodity by those in the cultural marketplace. But the bardic tradition holds that the artist creates on behalf of a people and at least attempts to speak for large proportions of that people in key moments.

Mishima's struggle with himself and with literature came to an end with *The Sea of Fertility* tetralogy in the late 1960s, which talks a great deal about small, conspiratorial groups of Right-wingers who contrive with elements of the post-Imperial Japanese military and General Staff to overthrow the business, corporate, and political elite of liberal, democratic Japan and reinstitute Emperor-worship. In one of his essays, Mishima asks, "Why did the Emperor have to become a human being?" because traditionally the Emperor was not regarded as human in Japan up until about 1945, '46, and thereafter.

Mishima made his last stand and his last statement in an East Tokyo army base on the 25th of November 1970, where, with either three or four acolytes from the Shield Society, and dressed in largely pre-1945 and Imperial Japanese military uniforms designed by himself, and with messages which were pithy statements of martial intent which Japanese warriors traditionally wear on their body. If you notice, in many Asiatic houses, there are often slogans or pieces of Buddhist scripture that are written calligraphically on the wall as either banners or forms of art, and they essentially adopt the position of a painting on the wall. Sometimes Japanese warriors write a slogan such as "Death is the Cardinal Reality" or something like that from the *Hagakure*, and fold it around their head with the Imperial emblem of Japan, which is the Sun.

The Shield Society, which was Mishima's own personal militaristic little society, numbering around a hundred persons, all of whom were supremely physically fit, all of whom were male, all of whom were invested with martial arts, had as its symbol two Imperial Japanese helmets from the seventeenth century cast in red and facing each other.

Mishima prepared banners and a proclamation which would be read out to the soldiers. He met, under a pretext of political falsity, General Mashita, who was in command of that particular East Tokyo army base. Swords and daggers — traditionally the samurai has a very long sword, he has two of them and he has two short or stabbing swords. In samurai warriorship, the culture of modern war, killing from a distance is disprivileged, even though of course in modern warfare, the Japanese army is highly organized and mechanistically capable and is as fully prepared to use modern weapons as anyone else. But interestingly, they dovetail these ancient and modern ideas with the cult of suicide and reckless personal death for an Imperial and popular mission. The cult of the kamikaze pilots, for example, who would dive their planes into American ships, causing massive explosions in their internal organs and workings and disable them and often destroy them in the Pacific theater of war, was part and parcel of that particular endeavor.

Mishima and his colleagues strode into Mashita's office, disarmed him, tied him up, produced some slogans on banners which they then draped from windows which led to a balcony outside this particular General's office, and then marched out to address the troops. About a thousand troops were lined up for some internal Japanese army matter, and it spread like wildfire that Mishima or somebody was acting in a strange or possibly terrorist manner in relation to this base. By the end of Mishima's speech to the troops, which was relatively short, helicopters were flying overhead in an attempt to disrupt what he was saying.

In his speech to the troops, which apart from its initial phase, when the troops stood in shocked silence, was received by jeers and hoots by the majority of them, Mishima demanded a return to the Empire of the Sun. He demanded a return to Empire-worship and to Imperial worship of the majesty of the Emperor. He demanded that the post-war Emperor would be declared *Tennō*, be declared a god again and be declared the god of the Japanese people. He also argued that the army cease to be American mercenaries, as he called it, and return to their traditional mission as the soul of Japan. He basically argued for a restoration of the Japanese war dead, and implicitly that the Japanese Emperor Hirohito at the time of the surrender in 1945 should have never denied his divinity or been forced to do so by American license, and should have accepted his responsibility as in Buddhism for the war dead. He essentially was demanding revisionism, the revision of the past and a sort of moral statement of victory in defeat which would allow the traditional Japan to resurface and to claim a form of spiritual conquest even after the bankruptcy of physical defeat in the atomic weapons used against its cities in the mid-1940s.

Mishima was really asking for the impossible, and asking for demands which the whole of contemporary Japan, with the exception of certain fringe far-Right and samurai groups, had set their face against.

Why did Mishima ask for these impossible demands which, to invent a term or a neologism, could be described as impossibilist demands? Many Western historians and literati believe that Mishima wanted to die and wished to commit suicide at this time, and used the call to arms of a renascent Imperial Japan based upon god-Emperor worship and the *kami* of the past as his excuse to commit *hari-kari*, or *seppuku*, in either Western or Japanese terms. This may have some psychological truth to it. Mishima was obsessed with death and with the morbid undercurrents of life and with the samurai cult of self-extinguishment from a very early age. He certainly had planned his suicide, and his will and his testamentary deposits over a year prior to the act. Every element of the act was thought through aesthetically.

After his speech was rejected by the body of the troops, he went back into the room and said various Shintoist prayers with his three or four colleagues. He then knelt down and ripped open his belly with one of the shorter of the samurai knives, which is the beginning of the ritual suicide in Japanese warrior culture. At the end of this act, your head is literally severed by another samurai who stands behind you. The head is then held aloft and then prayers are said over the head. His colleague committed ritual suicide in a similar way.

There is also a degree to which, as often happens in real life, the chosen associate of the suicide who later committed suicide himself couldn't go through with the act, and the stronger hand of a third samurai had to be used in order to inflict the beheading. The two heads were then placed next to each other, and ritual Buddhist and Shintoist prayers were said over the dead. This is because, in their belief system, of course, you are reincarnated as new life after forty days, and so this is not the end. It is a perpetuation of the prospect of a new beginning.

It is true to say that his ritual suicide and his demand for cultural revision and national reemergence caused a consternation in Japan. You have to understand he was the darling of the Eastern-Western media in Japan for quite a long period. He was also widely translated in an era when Japanese writers were not particularly widely translated. He was also widely popular inside Japan, despite being a self-consciously literary writer. And it literally caused consternation that he had done this. His revision and interpretative re-issue of the *Hagakure*, the bible of the samurai from three to four centuries before, became a bestseller in Japan after his funeral. Ten thousand ordinary Japanese, not associated with Right-wing groups or associated with nationalist caucuses or associated with samurai undercurrents inside or outside of the Japanese army at the time or associated with literary circles, attended Mishima's funeral, which was an event unheralded in the culture of the Japan at that time. It basically caused an enormous civic and psychological shock in Japan.

Was Mishima on a trajectory of his own? Did he represent the soul of his people, as he believed? Was his act a lonely and masochistic one totally contrary to the post-modern and Westernized wiles of contemporary Japan? Or was it in a sense a return, as he would have configured it, to fundamental verities about what it was to be Japanese, as against any other nationality on Earth?

Nobody really can come up with an answer. Possibly an answer is a medley of all of those questions put into one statement. A Westerner, certainly, is outside the remit of force and fire and the circle of the Sun which is necessary to ponder such questions.

But there is a degree to which most of Yukio Mishima's major works have been translated into English, including *Confessions of a Mask, Sun and Steel, Madame de Sade, My Friend Hitler, On the Heroic War Dead of the Japanese Nation, The Temple of the Golden Pavilion, Forbidden Colors, The Sea of Fertility* tetralogy, and many others. And the interesting thing about them is they often deal with a decadent violence and an amorality, such as in *The Sailor Who Fell from Grace with the Sea,* unless the samurai ethic is put underneath them and those sort of yearnings for violence and for order which he sees in traditional, pre-modern, pre-Second World War versions of Japanese society are re-institutionalized.

MAURICE COWLING:
ULTRA-CONSERVATIVE EXTRAORDINAIRE*

I have been asked to talk about various things, but I would like to talk about Maurice Cowling particularly, who I call an ultra-conservative extraordinaire. Professor Cowling's dead now. But he was a very interesting man. He crossed over all sorts of theoretical boundaries in his career as an academic and, I suppose, a sort of radical conservative journalist for many years.

Now, I knew him about ten to fifteen years before his death, and he taught at Peterhouse. There's this novel by C. P. Snow called *The Masters* about an election in a Cambridge college, Oxbridge College, on the intensity of the political passions at the microscopic level amongst these clever men. And that is very much the sort of ambience in which this man moved. He was regarded in some ways as a little bit of a Thatcherite. He never was. And I always had the impression that like Professor Roger Scruton, who he was different from but who he resembled in certain respects, he is often wheeled out when people wish to damage the mainstream Conservative and Unionist Party.

It was well said that in the 1980s that Penguin, a book publisher not particularly friendly to the Tories, published two books, Milton Friedman's *Free to Choose*, the bible of Chicago School libertarian capitalism, and Roger Scruton's *The Meaning of Conservatism*. And they did both of those in some ways to attack the Conservative Party of that time. But no one would accuse you of attacking anything when you're publishing intellectual material that is in some way adjacent to the party concerned.

Now, Maurice Cowling was a very radical individual in all

---

* This lecture was delivered at the first meeting of the Society of National Conservatives on September 21, 2009. The transcript was made by V. S. with special thanks to D. K.

sorts of ways. I'll say a few biographical things about him first, because he's just an interesting man. The first thing is that Cowling lived at night, that Cowling would sleep during the day, and he'd sit up at night. When you had a university seminar with him, you'd go and see him at one in the morning. Everybody was sort of wrecked, essentially, when they climbed up to this tower to see him, and the mist would be coming out of the Cam. And the porter would open . . . It's like the scene in *Macbeth* with the porter, after the murder when he's got the chains on the door, and you come in there, and this leery old porter looks at you and says, "Professor Cowling, is it, sir?" And you say, "Yes."

You go up this stairwell, and you open the door, and Cowling will be in this book-lined room, straight out of scenes with Jonathan Harker in *Dracula*, you know? You go into this room, and there's books on this wall and books on this wall and books on this wall, and Cowling's lying on the bed dressed in green. And you go in there, and he looks at you, and he says, "Oh, it's you again." In Cambridge, you have to read the SAR. He taught political philosophy: Aristotle, Heraclitus, Plato to Hobbes, libertarianism, and in some respect John Rawls, in a way, but it's that sort of spectrum.

And he would give you these essays that didn't really relate to the course as such, but you had to do a certain amount of work for it. In a way, you were more than educated to sort of get the degree. He wasn't particularly concerned with qualifications. On Marx and Engels, he'd just invent an essay for you and say, "Marx: apocalyptian libertarian. Discuss." And he'd have you go away and do that. And of course, what he's talking about is the 1844 manuscripts, the early Marx, the differentiation from the scientific socialism that comes later.

The interesting thing about Cowling is that Cowling was a sort of archetype for the sort of dons depicted in *Porterhouse Blue* by Tom Sharpe, because of course in that comedy, Porterhouse means Peterhouse, and he's talking about the ultra-reactionaries in Cambridge.

Now, Cowling was deeply un-English in certain respects and deeply English in others. When I say un-English, he was

ultra-intellectual, had no time for small talk: drivel and garbage! [unintelligible] Now, if you made an intellectual proposition, or you wrote a sentence down in your essay—because you
had to read it out loud in front of him—and he [unintelligible]
it, he would attack everything you've said. He would attack
every proposition and he would attack every idea behind it,
because he believed in dialectics. He believed that struggle is
the meaning of truth. So, you had this war with him basically
between about 1:30 and quarter of 3 in the morning, and then
you'd stagger down the tower, and another victim would come
up to be impaled, and you'd see him sneaking up the stairs.

It was well-known that female students had to be kept away
from him. Not for the usual reasons, but because he was so intellectually merciless that it was sort of damaging. Certain students had to be kept away from him as well, so they only used
to throw into the gladiatorial pit of combat the ones who could
take it. And this tells you a lot about Maurice, in that Maurice
was a sort of somewhat slightly dangerous man, certainly for
the sort of academic life of that era.

I remember George Steiner, the Emeritus Professor of European culture and civilization at Churchill and at Geneva University simultaneously, [unintelligible] Cambridge, once said at
a private party that he regarded Maurice Cowling as evil and a
force for evil, and there are various reasons why he might think
that, personal and otherwise.

Now, Maurice Cowling is unusual in that he was a deeply
elitist and extreme conservative, and a very intellectually assiduous individual. The interesting thing about him is that he
set himself in a more Continental way against liberalism as a
conception. He didn't think of conservatism as a species of liberalism. He thought of conservatism as in some respects an anti-Enlightenment proposition.

He didn't quite do a thesis or PhD in the usual way, but his
basic thesis text, a bit like Nietzsche's *The Birth of Tragedy*, was
about John Stuart Mill and was published to general horror
several years later. He sort of launched himself into an attack
upon Mill. His argument about him is quite eccentric even
from the perspective of people who don't care for that particu-

lar thinker, because his view was that contrary to the idea that Mill was opening up towards tolerance and inclusion and freedom of thought and freedom of belief and secularity and a sort of plenitude of milky goodness, he regarded him as an implicit totalitarian, a prig, a man determined to impose his values and views on others and a militant destroyer of religion and an aggressive secularist.

One of Cowling's theses is that liberalism isn't a nice viewpoint as everyone imagines, but actually is a devouring viewpoint, particularly of prior religious ideas that uphold notions of hierarchy in society. So, his second book was on the use and misuse/limitations of political science. Cowling's early books were very abstract, and were one of the reasons he basically resumed after a break in his academic career.

His career was broken by war, the Second World War, and broken by a period in journalism. But he could never really get started in journalism because he always had a tendency to write scathing reviews [unintelligible] journal, or to attack the editor, or to [unintelligible] in print, and you can only imagine, because he was such a cross-grained "reactionary" and difficult individual that, very like Auberon Waugh, a journalist who in many ways he resembles. Auberon Waugh once wrote an article in *The Spectator* in 1974 arguing for a *coup d'etat* in Britain, which didn't make him incredibly popular. But then again, who wants to be popular? And Cowling was a bit similar. He was sacked, or "removed," the expression was, from the Express Group, because the editors said, "You're too reactionary, even for us." This was in the early '60s, which in many ways was quite prior to the cultural and social deluge which was to occur.

So he resumes his academic career with these texts in the background on Mill and on the uses of politics. And in a strange way for such a theoretical man, the belief that theory doesn't impinge upon the life and manners and mores of politicians very much.

Cowling was a very complex individual, because although he believed that intellectual ideas dominate life, and intellectuals are the power class, even though they have no formal pow-

er in our society, because everybody else is so dumb and beneath them and the level of their ideas. He believed that politicians are usually motivated by everything other than principles.

And Cowling is a strange individual, because although he
had preferred beliefs of his own, he was also a little bit of a nihilist. He was essentially an attacker. He had a mind that is often more associated with the Left than the Right, because
whenever you put a proposition to him his first idea will be to
attack, to deconstruct, to break down, to sweep away, and to
see if your ideas could stand it. It's a sort of slightly more aggressive version of the Socratic method whereby you don't put
forward your own proposition, you just chisel away at whatever anyone has said to you and remain somehow to one side,
you know? Of course, he had no Plato to explicate it all even
better than he may have put it at the time later, so he had to do
that for himself.

So, you've got this strange tension in Cowling between an
ultra-theoretical view of life and the view that politicians are
deliberative rogues acting in microscopic ways, particularly in
relation to loyalties that they have with each other within cabi-
nets, within parties, and within bureaucracies. Like Enoch
Powell, he believed, in particularly English and British terms,
that party was very important, and he was completely dis-
missive of the modern idea that they're all the same and what
does it matter which party people are in. He liked the idea of
the good party man, even though he didn't associate with
them, because they were a bore.

Cowling regarded most people as bores, including Michael
Portillo, whom he educated and who many people think he
groomed mentally for the leadership of the Tory Party. But
when somebody would ask Cowling, "What's your view of
Michael Portillo?" he'd say, "Oh well, he'd make a middling
bureaucrat in a private business." He was always slightly con-
descending about everyone, really, including most of his fellow
dons.

Just to engage in a little, sort of *ad hominem* remarks, one of
his favorite sparring partners was Hugh Trevor-Roper, who

committed a major *faux pas* when he authenticated the Hitler diaries. It was an enormous scandal that went around the world. And Cowling set up a dinner party in Cambridge called The Authenticators, and everybody had to put up their hand when they went to his dinner party and say, "I totally authenticate, with my heart, the proven efficacy of these texts. I know he wrote them, and I put my entire reputation upon it!" Which was some stupid thing that Roper had come out with in the furor, when *Stern* had been had, and paid twelve million deutschmarks, or whatever they paid, to some elderly German forger, who forged multiple volumes of this stuff with his own calligraphic set in his garage. They paid millions and millions for this. The only historian, interestingly, who said that they were fakes from beginning to end was David Irving. Life has a funny way of behaving, because a couple weeks ago I went to a garden party that Irving gave in which he talked about these and other matters, and I suddenly appeared [unintelligible] with many others appearing at this garden party. To go to a Buckinghamshire garden party, on a Sunday, it's the basest of all infamy, isn't it, really?

Now, Cowling had this sort of rivalry with Trevor-Roper, who of course was regarded as something of a Third Reich expert because he wrote the famous book about the Bunker, *The Last Days of Hitler*. But he brawled with all other academics, really, because of his nature. Despite all the comedy and the element of a C. P. Snow reactionary don lookalike, he wrote three, four, five very, very serious intellectual books. So serious that most of his conservative students who passed, put under his "care," didn't entirely realize what he was saying.

My view of Cowling is that the idea that he was a mainstream historian, whereas someone like Irving is a demon, is in many ways false. I would say, in some respects, Cowling is to the right of Irving. This is one of the paradoxes that you face in late modernity, where certain people are regarded as beyond the pale of the pale of the pale, and other people are regarded as quite mainstream, and it's actually partly because no one ever really looks at their ideas.

Irving's a nostalgic. He would love this country to be like

the 1950s. His *faux pas* is that he's sort of fallen in love with Adolf Hitler, which as a historian is regarded as not such a brilliant move, if you want to be published by Macmillan, which he was, of course, earlier in his career. Martin Gilbert hates Hitler and loves Churchill, and he's sort of inverted it, hasn't he, you know? He would have been with Churchill's wife burning a prominent modernist portrait of Churchill downstairs at the charcoal oven, chopping it up and using it as firewood. You know what Churchill said about that painting? He said, "It makes me look thick, and I ain't."

But Cowling is very, very Right-wing, but in a complicated way. He had no time for Continental ultra-Right-wing views. He believed that the key to the radical and absolutist Right in Britain is it never really said what it is. And it must come from inside the brain of the Tory Party, and he would educate those brains before they entered the cabinet. This is his central theory.

His first book was about the Labour government in 1924 leading to Labour's involvement in the administration prior to the crash of 1929, the so-called betrayal of the labor movement and the emergence of some national Labour people around Ramsay MacDonald, and their adoption [unintelligible] into what was essentially a Conservative administration. Now, Cowling was pathologically opposed to Labour's influence in modern twentieth-century life because he basically didn't believe that the masses should have democratic representation in the way that they've got it. He wasn't a democrat particularly, and he believed in the manipulation of state power by little conservative elites. He believed that Labour would always push everything, even within democratic norms, further and further to the Left because it was the logic of their position.

By further and further to the Left, he means to make more equal. Because Cowling realized, in the way that really only Continental far Right thinkers like Benoist realized, that the real point about the Right isn't concepts like race or religion or nationality, although clearly these are very significant, it's inequality — it's the spiritual goodness, if you like, of inequality as the founding belief and structure. All of the others are discourses — certainly this is how he configured them — or semiotics through which you or by virtue of which you build meaning through inequality.

Therefore, he was the sort of conservative, or ultraconservative, call it what you will, who believed that the maximization of inequality, not just material inequality, which is a very low form of inequality, or equality, but immaterial forms of equality/inequality are what life is about. Hierarchies of beauty, of form, of intellect, of knowledge. These are of course aristocratic, pre-democratic, anti-middle class, anti-bourgeois class, illiberal conceptions; even though he comes from that background himself, a lot like Nietzsche in a differentiated way, he became spokesman for aristocratic mores in a British setting.

This book about the Labour administration in 1924, which is called *The Impact of Labour*, is incredibly detailed. The Left-wing historian, A. J. P. Taylor, said that, "Of all the historians of his generation, Cowling had the greatest mind, after my own." You can't beat them, can you? But Taylor who, of course, was one of the founding members of the CND [Campaign for Nuclear Disarmament] and was on the Committee of 100, the most radical element of the CND with Bertrand Russell and all these people who all sat in front of the nuclear power plants, all sat in front of the American nuclear bunkers, all sat in front of the Ministry of Defence on Northumberland Avenue. What they thought they'd achieve by sitting in the rain, other than dirtying their backs, one doesn't really know. But that's what A. J. P. Taylor thought.

Taylor himself was a dissident, of course, who wrote a soft revisionist book about the origins of the Second World War called, with devastating unoriginality, *The Origins of the Second World War*, which caused immense difficulty and was denounced from all circles. And when the ferocious denunciations of Taylor came in, Taylor would run to the postbox and go, "Look, there's another one!" Because he actively loved this sort of gadfly madness.

Now, his view of Cowling's work is very interesting because it comes from the other side, politically, and Cowling would concentrate on the micro-politics of Labour figures: where they came from, which chapel they went to, what denomination within Christianity they did or didn't believe in, whether they were an atheist or not, internally or externally, and whether their religious belief was just purely social or whether it had a theological basis. These are key elements for Cowling, but also the alliances that people form. Unlike a lot of academic and purely theoretical historians [unintelligible] Even Marxist historians like Hobsbawm or E. P. Thompson, for example, are deeply empirical in relation to a lot of Continental writers, because that seems to be the British historiographical tradition, of which Cowling was definitely an exponent.

The interesting thing is the outer scope and texture of power and how these politicians behave, particularly under stress, because they're nearly always under stress in one way or another. And his view is that when you allow a sentiment into the state, they will have to spend money; they will have to go off the gold standard; they have to introduce social provisions for the masses; they have to take care of the people that the Tories don't regard sociologically as part of their nation. They're there to do that. This means there will be inflation. This means that the economic divisions between the classes will lessen. This means you will have a more egalitarian society whether you like it or not. Other people say that's inevitable, given the access of the masses into modernity in the twentieth century.

Later on, although they were in the same decade, Cowling writes another book after *Impact of Labour* and this is called *The Impact of Hitler*. And this is British foreign policy. This is probably his most controversial book, really, and the one for which he's widely known for outside of purely academic circles. *The Impact of Hitler: British Diplomacy and Foreign Policy, 1933–1940*. It's a very provocative book in many ways. All of these books were published for the most part by Cambridge University Press or the University of Chicago, which brought out a well-known edition of this particular book.

The thesis of this book is that the British were reacting to the emergence of ferocious new Caesarisms, which is how Cowling looked at fascism on the European continent in the 1920s and

1930s in various ways. What really mattered were the national factions within the leadership of the Conservative Party. Don't forget that everyone who knows anything about the history of this country during the '30s knows, Churchill and his group were complete outsiders during that period and were regarded as semi-lunatics and wild men. It used to be said by ordinary Tories in the mid-'30s, "You're not one of those ghastly Churchill men, are you?" You know, when they met people who they thought might be, because Churchill was an outsider and he wanted to make trouble and wanted another enormous bloodbath with Germany, which much of that whole generation was determined to prevent occurring, given the fact that they might have fought in the first one between 1914–18 or lived through it, or relatives of theirs died in it, and so on.

What Cowling's thesis is, which is deeply unpleasant in relation to mainstream center-Right opinion now, although he was never a man who was really bothered whether people thought he was pleasant or not—there was a degree to which he thinks the whole history of the Second World War and what followed it has been ludicrously sentimentalized—and he's a totally unsentimental individual who hopes to try to see that they remain clear—and also that it's been written from a Labour point of view.

In other words, the view of the Atlee administration, the view of people who were in opposition, and in quite minor opposition, up until the national government of '39-'40, essentially Chamberlain, had completely failed. When they came in . . . the radicals in the Labour Party, people like the young Michael Foot, who wrote this book/chapbook/pamphlet called *Guilty Men*, the appeasers . . .

He thinks that Labour conquered the mental space in Britain long before they formed the absolute majority-elected dictatorship, which is how he sees democracy, between 1945 and 1951. Labour, of course, through the Nationality Act of 1948, begins the process of mass immigration initially from the old Empire or the Commonwealth, which results in the society we have now. So, Cowling believed that Labour is crucial in its replacement of the Liberal Party as the center-Left opposition within the British state and its regime.

The interesting thing is that a lot of Cowling's analysis of politics is Machiavellian in the sense that power and self-interest on behalf of wider groups are what politics is about. He doesn't believe in any of the nicer and more moral constructions that people do it for others, that they do it for the esteem of others, or have for them, that they do it in order to serve the public good, as John Major once said. He'd regard that as tawdry rubbish put forward by a miserable loser. So, his view of everything is sort of slightly ferocious and acidic.

But his analysis of this country's decline, which is a sort of internalized and microscopic version of Correlli Barnett's thesis in *The Collapse of British Power*, which deals with the same events in a more narrative-based, wider, less narrow, historical contingent. Both very similar. Both upper middle class, actually upper-class men, both ultraconservatives of [unintelligible] British culture, both outsiders in relation to the Britain which had already been created by the middle of the last century, never mind before.

Don't be fooled by the fact, as many Leftists would, that there are lots of blue-blooded people who still run structures in this society. The class that once ruled in this country until about 1920 is gone. And when it's gone like in the Soviet Union, or previously like in revolutionary France two hundred years before, but they're gone, and it's now a mass bourgeois, liberal society, which in his way of looking at things has been ethically and culturally proletarianized. And that's what you have, if you take away the cant and the soft words. So, that's the thesis of that book.

The other thing about the book that shocked a lot of commentators at the time is that there's no moral judgment about fascism. Hitler's seen as a ruthless leader, growing up on the streets in post-war, post-1918 Germany, six million German unemployed, men rotting in doorways, men without feet, men living in cardboard boxes. He offered them hope; he offered them vengeance; he offered them a little group to hate and blame it all on. He regarded it as axiomatic. [unintelligible] The Germans aren't meant to have democracy anyway. These are views which are almost never even expressed now. There's also the idea that in a sense that movement represented Prussianism from the street, the return of the Second Reich in a very virile, forceful way because it in some ways lacked the polish of the old elite.

In many ways, as a Briton, he was able to figure [unintelligible] in his analysis of that era and of that particular movement, which in many ways has become the most notorious movement of the twentieth century, hasn't it really, even today. Even though it was completely defeated and obliterated in 1945. It's strange how it's still alive, at least in the mental state that swirls around. More people couldn't tell you who de Gaulle was, couldn't tell you who Roosevelt was. More people know who some supermodel is dating than who was Prime Minister in 1940. But they all know about that particular dictator. It's quite strange how it's gone outside history and become sort of part of the generalized psychopomp and mass culture. And it's always a sign for the historian if they don't play those sort of demonic games and if they adopt a hard-headed, unsentimental attitude. Many liberals believe they adopt that attitude because they're slightly sympathetic to it. In the case of someone like Alan Clark, who Cowling knew very well, that was not a completely uncharitable view, to be frank.

Now, Cowling wrote this book in which he basically said we should not have fought Germany — and he later [unintelligible] in a *Sunday Telegraph* article — we should have done peacefully in 1941 after we were defeated in France, we should've been left to one side, we would have kept the Empire, and we would have turned east mercilessly against Stalinist Communism and probably defeated it without another front. This was a revisionist, a soft revisionist, thesis, but a very revisionist one for which he was demonized and subject to quite a degree of opprobrium. But if you live at heights, in a tower, at a Cambridge college, these brickbats of outraged polytechnic thoughts don't really shatter your windows, do they? So you only heard it in a muffled roar in the distance, really.

That was certainly the most "demonic" and "near the edge" work Cowling ever did. It's interesting to note that it was sold by all sorts of groups all over the world, way beyond the portals of the University of Chicago Press or Cambridge University Press. The most extreme National Socialist organization in the United States, which was called the National Alliance, and was led by William Pierce, actually sold Maurice Cowling's *The Impact of Hitler*. He understood intellectually where it was coming from, even in a dissentient way.

So, in a way, Cowling is prepared to be heretical. Cowling is prepared to do what soft Leftists do. They basically say, "No enemies on the Left." And when Clare Short once said, when Communism had been destroyed, "Communism has gone down, but Marxism has not been beaten." That, in many ways, is the difference between the Left and the Right, that moderate Leftists who do not like the politics of Communism, its harshness, totalitarianism, its viciousness, [unintelligible]. They're like O'Brien from *Nineteen Eighty-Four*. But they are prepared to look at, to think about, and to use the theoretical ideas of an enormous range of Marxists, from Gramsci to Adorno to [unintelligible] and so on. They're not frightened of ideas.

Whereas the conservative tradition, largely, you know, Scruton and Oakeshott are all right, but if you go any further out than that, it's regarded as terrifying, and you are supping with the Devil. And you have to have a very long spoon in order to do that. So, in a sense, he's reacting against that type of hypocrisy, the idea that some ideas are respectable and others are not. Where, as far as he was concerned, they're all ideas. And many of them mask the urgency of power.

Now, one particular claim which certain liberals were not slow to make, they certainly were, considering he was a man who debated life, was that there's a sort of nihilistic structuralism to this. That in a way, what are the absolutes that he believes in? I once said that he was a Tory like this, and he just laughed, which is sort of an endorsement, and there's a complicated element going on there. Although he believed that socialized religion was inevitable, was necessary to hold civilization together, and its loss through secular erosion and relativism in this society was what's led to what we've got, that was his view. How firm his own beliefs were in high Anglican

Christianity is difficult to say, but of course there are Right-wing forms of personalized skepticism or atheism or just non-committal, they keep it private, which are different to the Left-wing and liberal versions of those forms.

The leader of French integral nationalism in the twentieth century, Charles Maurras, leading a French fundamentalist neo-Catholicism really, he was in all probability an atheist. Why? Because certain people of his temper can't believe themselves, they don't believe that the structure of their civilization should be torn down just because they have a prior disbelief. So, they are constructivists.

In other words, they don't believe that all of history is reducible to my consciousness about it at a particular moment, because one's part of an interconnected continuum that pre-exists one and that will post-date one, and so although one's private views are important to ourselves and one's circle, and so on, they are not necessarily culturally determining factors. And that's an interesting attitude, because it means that even people who are skeptical about the Christian inheritance, which you could say is the vast majority of socialist-minded and liberal-minded and [unintelligible] intellectuals and their feminist and other [unintelligible] later, all were, doesn't necessarily mean that you have to then go on to believe that you tear the whole thing down.

Enoch Powell, who had a little bit of a parallel career inside politics to Cowling, both ultra-intellectual, both spare, both slightly puritanical men, both ascetic, both very hard-minded in the nature of their personal discourse and thinking. Just mind to mind. Powell could speak ten languages and wrote ten to twenty academic books, and yet didn't really have a proper academic career and just loved burning people. His last book at the end about Christ being stabbed rather than crucified, was just to annoy all sorts of people he knew. Because they're gad-flies, these sorts of people. They do like causing trouble, and that's just part of who and what they are.

And there's an interesting parallelism at another level, though. Powell was very influenced by Nietzsche when he was young. Very much so. And, sort of, the ruthlessness and ferocity of that thinking, and the fanaticism of that thinking certainly appealed to him emotionally, although he later softened and moved away from it. And Cowling was never sort of formally influenced by Nietzsche, because part of him had a distaste for Continental Europeans in that very old English, sort of British, way, even though mentally he was very aware of their achievements, but he could argue [unintelligible] Nietzsche [unintelligible] and that was part of his strength. So, he once said to me, "I don't mind a spot of bigotry, you know? As long as it's in a good cause." There were always sort of John Taylor-type [unintelligible] that were always there in the background, because he regarded them as having nerve rather than just a floating sort of semi-visual definition of identity.

One of the things that's very important about all these figures is that they're great characters. One thing you'll notice about English and British life now is how levelled down people are. The great, monstrous characters of the past seem fewer and fewer, and many of the attitudes that they had—their crankiness, their difficulty, their indomitable character, and so on— seems to have disappeared as well. It needs some particular mention how Cowling, Powell . . . You had these sorts of figures. [unintelligible] There's just no way around it.

Now, on the positive side, not what you're against and what you deconstruct, but what you build, Cowling went back to a Christian position. "Went back" may not be the correct term, because he may not have really renounced it in the way Powell did earlier, so it was less of a mental moving back. But still, his last three books, which appeared in the 1980s, 1990s, and the first year of this decade (2001), were books about the Anglican Church and its ideas and its ideology as he perceived it, its theological praxis.

Don't forget this is a church, which in many ways is a combination of different things. A bit of [unintelligible], a bit of national compromise, it contains the Protestant anti-clerical element, it contains semi-rationalist Protestant clerisy that's establishmentarian and almost has no beliefs except the prism of power with a morality in the background, has an Anglo-Catholic wing, of course, some of whom have formally left for the Roman Church now, and it's a medley from a hardline theological point of view. It's a dog's breakfast of an organization really, for political reasons, where the Protestants and the Catholics pull at either end, but those that align against the liberals within the church dislike them more than each other, and all that, you know.

In some ways it's a perfect organization to express Cowling's view of life, where ideas are in the background. Some people are purely animated by them, but they are very rare, and even most of them are lying to themselves and being rather puppet-like, sort of view of the way things happen.

But, in actual fact, his three books, which if I were to put all of them on the bar here would be at least this high, all three of them . . . And yet, it seems such a dry subject, the internal high, high politics of the semi-aristocratic leadership of the Anglican Church for one hundred fifty years. Most young undergraduates would be gagging just at that description, and yet it's a fascinating collection of books, because the characters of these men, the intellectual violence of their disputes, the belief that they influence the inner mindset of the inner elite of the Empire's last days, and that's what Cowling's concerned about.

He's not concerned about what the masses believe. The masses believe what they're told to believe. He's a pure elitist. Eighty percent of people have no ideas. They just conform to the political correctness of the hour. They conform to the liberal humanist PC rhetoric now, which screams over the telly towards them and in every other media, because they are going to conform to whatever view. They would have conformed, as they did in the past, to a national, semi-racial, patriotic, old-style view of Britain, which is now regarded by many people as a slightly monstrous attitude, although probably in his heart, it's what people like Cowling and Powell really believed about this country in fact, and it's just a truthful statement.

Now, these books are deconstructivist texts, in my opinion. These books are his attempt to put forward his agenda. The dilemma he's facing, of course, is almost complete liberal takeover of the mental space of the Anglican Church. But, of course, because he believes that ideas dominate the mind, and

the mind is a subconscious of the brain, and therefore what
elite brains think is of importance way out of proportion to the
small number of people they talk to and write for. Because he
believes, rather like Shelley, who said that poets are the
unacknowledged legislators of mankind, he believed that people who produced theories through with which all the other
middling minds speak and think control the agenda. They
don't control it in any personal way. It's not their property. But
they control the remit and the nature of the debate.

The total collapse of Anglicanism into liberalism, the total
collapse into secular humanism whereby almost any Christian
element is completely removed, whereas the important thing
about religion to the Cowlings of this world is its mysticism, is
its irrationalism, its appeal to that which is beyond and therefore can't be argued about, its hieratic possibilities, that element that says, "Believe!" and is beyond debate. So, you have
this strange element, which is always the paradox of the intellectual, particularly the [unintelligible] intellectual position,
that a man who is as theoretical as anyone you could ever meet
ends up justifying the organicism of belief and the leap into
faith, as Kierkegaard would have it, beyond any possibility of
complete rational gainsaying, denial, equivocation, or mis-
statement.

You come back irreducibly in all Right-wing thinking to,
"What are you to base hierarchy upon?" What do you base the
possibility of transcendence within hierarchy upon? Brute
force? Law? Systems of faith? If a system of faith, what system
of faith and why and how are people to believe in it at the level
of an elite, an intermediate or middling group (very important
in modern societies, of course; now dominant, culturally) and
the majority? And how do you hold these people together?
And what for? And Cowling would be Machiavellian enough
to say, "And what lies do you need to tell them to hold it together?" Because he believed politics was partly about that.

He used to always get very contemptuous when people
used to say, "Politics is such a higher . . ." because they're such
frauds! And he would say, "Look, they are moving within a
vortex of power where they have to face off against three or

four different tendencies, some of which may resort—certainly outside of this country and speaking of a few years back—to physical violence. And there's no proving of truth in that area. That's not what they're for. That's the role of a philosopher, or a philosopher-king in the Platonic sense, not a British cabinet minister in the 1930s."

I once asked him what his view of the extreme Right was, and he said, "What, you mean people like Mosley?" I said, "Yes." And he said, "Well, they are essentially movements that are cut off from what I consider the Right to be." And Oswald Mosley came from the inner aristocracy, of course. And he said, "When you go outside Parliament, when you go outside the structures of the British establishment," this is his thinking, you go into the working class, you go into the masses, and they never have any power. They can create a lot of force, but they never have come to power in our country.

During the Revolution, the one of the political sort we had four hundred years ago, the masses were energized just for a small moment, and then the dictatorship closed, once the monarchy had been removed. And once the dictator was dead, his son was put in by the army council. They realized he was a fool and a weakling, and they got the monarchy back very quickly.

Cowling approved of that. These radical Parliamentarians and Puritans and ideologues of the day realized there was no strong man to hold it together, so they immediately opened up to the old order again and said, "Take it back. There will be no recriminations. There will be no show trials." The man who stood for the execution of one king stood to salute another one coming in.

That was the elixir of Englishness as Cowling regarded it. The ability to, even in very theoretical minds, people with very theoretical and intellectual minds, put that intellect on no account in moments of national strife and to embrace the reasons which in a way are sometimes purely physiological and irrational, viewed in liberal, rational humanist terms where every decision that every person makes is based upon a rational calculation of utility, of outcome, the moral notion that is very consequent to liberal thinking now, philosophically and ethically, called consequentialism, whereby all that ever matters is the consequences of a particular action. The total reversal of the prior religious view that what matters is intention.

If you run a child over and you didn't mean to, it's manslaughter, which is punished in most Western European countries in a quite minor way. Tell that to the mother of the child that's been run over. Whereas, if it could be proven that intentionally the driver put his foot down because he'd been writing on a blog how he disliked that child and this sort of thing, and there's intention there, then that is completely different and is perceived as such. So, if you have intention of mind behind an action . . . From the religious view, everything is prior, and the more radical the religiosity, the more the meaning of life is determined before one even starts thinking about how one might agree or disagree with that.

The liberal view that you have a heuristic way of looking at things, you make them up as you go along, that everything's relative in relation to everything else, that life is existential and not essential is the opposite of what he believed. And so, in a strange way, you end up with very theoretical, very abstract ideas based upon empiricism, based upon deep historical knowledge of texts and analysis of the psychological motivations of individual politicians and clerics, most of whom no one's ever heard of.

Now, Cowling died a couple years ago and got some major obituaries in *The Times* and *The Telegraph*. A rare [unintelligible]. He certainly, in my view, misunderstood that the libertarians who had largely taken over the Tory Party in the post-war period, although he would have analyzed them quite correctly as extremist liberals of a different sort. He didn't quite realize that the ruthlessness and the ability to shape-shift and change positions, which has seen Michael Portillo morph from an allegedly Right-wing Tory Defence Minister and hate figure of the Left, to Diane Abbott's best mate, and they sit together on a divan in a television studio. It's a strange transformation to occur. Cowling would actually be amazed by the extraordinary cynicism in such a move for a man who professed hard-edged, no-nonsense, cynicism, and a complete sort of spare, unshuffling attitude towards things. That's an interesting parallel.

The cynicism of what intellectuals call ordinary people can often take the breath away from an intellectual cynic. That's an interesting conceit. Just as intellectuals can change their positions so quickly in a way that bedazzles people who are not dominated by ideas.

I know I reacted in what is called a salon when I was 18, and I realized that people who call themselves intellectuals had their own class system. They'd talk about intellectuals and ordinary people. Who are these ordinary people? I suddenly realized the word was divided for them into those that lived purely the life of the mind and the rest. All groups have their inclusions and their exclusions because you can't have a discourse without it. All groups rely on ordering who's in the group, who's outside the group, and so on.

So, I think he misinterpreted the changes in the Conservative Party, which in some ways was his great hope. His great hope was that the Conservative Party has no views. The Conservative Party just *is*. And therefore, in his way of looking at it, anyone can come to power within it. He'd be very displeased with me. He'd say, "You've been a fool. You've been too honest. Honesty is never a good idea in politics, ever." This is his view. He said, "You should have completely hidden what your actual views are." He said, "You've been mingling with extremist politicians and gone out to the fringes. You should have stayed inside and chiseled your way out." This is his way of thinking, I think.

But the problem with that view, and this has happened to legions of Tory MPs and others, is in the old days they could have their little groups like the Monday Club and so on, on the Right-wing of the Tory Party. Those views don't even exist anymore. [unintelligible] When Iain Duncan Smith became leader, and the Party voted for him to be leader because he resembled the people who are voters of the Party, and they wanted him. And then they realized his sort of rough sense of humor of this block of wood, you know, and was sort of completely unelectable in mass terms. And there was a coup. All the politicians got together in the Commons, never mind the public.

They had a coup to get Howard in, because he was just a bit freer with the medium.

And in a strange sort of way, that sort of palace killing was the sort of politics that Cowling lived and breathed, but I think he misunderstood the importance of mass society. In late modernity, he overestimated the corridors of power and the influence of a tiny, little, microscopic elite and the divisions between them. I think, possibly, before 1924 — and don't forget most of his books are written in a politics that precedes the modern world as we conceive it now — his way of looking at things was much more salient. But now I think increasingly it doesn't matter. I consider this country as ruled by one party. And it has three wings, and the Liberal Democrats in the middle. They swivel and provide the ideas for the other two blocs, although they can't ever get in, except in some [unintelligible] way.

And the blocs are class-based: center-Right, the south of England and environs, and the bourgeois class; center-Left the north of England, southern Wales, bigger cities, and so on. And they move around each other, but ideologically, all of these parties pushed together believe in eighty percent . . . They're all secularists; they're all humanists; they're all egalitarian to a degree; they're all in favor of the EU; they're all in favor of multiculturalism; they're all in favor of migration. You have multiculturalism because you have migration, not the other way around, and so on. As you go out towards the margins of the Labour Party, the American domination of the consensus as it is, that becomes more rancid, that becomes more adversarial, and the people just drop away there, that is true. And there are other areas where that meme or model — particular models always break down in human affairs — but the point I was speaking, that's true, we're ruled by one party with three wings. And I don't think he really grasped that.

So, like all political thinkers and political philosophers, there's a sort of Wagnerian moment at the end, you know? He sat with Enoch Powell in South Down when he lost that seat in Northern Ireland over Paisleyites in the Democratic Unionist Party, who are now the hegemonic party amongst the Unionists in Northern Ireland. Running a candidate against him purely to defeat him. Because they didn't like him, because he was an Englishman, and an outsider, and somebody who advocated fusion with the rest of Britain where they wanted to devolve Protestant power inside Ulster. All these divisions, that don't matter anything really to people over here, but for them it's absolutely crucial! Powell sat there, watching the votes, watching the baggage of his whole political career, his decades as an MP. He said that, "All political careers end in failure."

And of course, that is true. That is a true viewpoint, metaphysically. Because broadly speaking, with the exception of the most radically totalitarian elements within fascistic ideas, the Right is anti-utopian. Look at you people. You're not capable of perfection. And all attempts to do that are a Procrustean affair, essentially. [unintelligible] That is, ultimately, the most radical Left-wing line. And so, in a sense, a slightly morbid and pessimistic attitude towards human folly and the imperfection of political structures is Right-wing.

Cowling's influence, I think, is interesting because despite his beliefism, despite the fact that very few people outside of academic life have heard of him, despite the fact that he's a difficult and cryptic customer, on the page and in life, he does point to one interesting thing, and that's the combination of metaphysical conservatism and Right-wing radicalism with pure theory, the rejection of pessimism and anti-intellectuality, which are largely associated with conservatives to many people, particularly on the Left. Many people I knew joined Left-wing groups when they were young, because they thought the Right wasn't interesting and wasn't interested in ideas. Don't forget many people's ideas are quite superficial. Why do you think that . . . when I was at university the Left dominated everything. Absolutely everything. Now the Left, in a hard-Left form, is very small and very attenuated.

I knew a lecturer in sociology at the polytechnic in North London, one of the most Left-wing institutions in Britain, and at that time we found [unintelligible] in North London, where all must have degrees. Degrees in golf, degrees in hairstyling, degrees in peanut butter, you know. You fill in a form and get a PhD in nuclear physics back by [unintelligible]. Fifty percent will have degrees soon. That's what Brown wants. You know, that's the way it's going. And, of course, if you look at it, the sort of academicism that Cowling represented was the complete reverse of that. He would have advocated less universities. He said to me, "The polys are just for training people to fix cars! Get rid of a few of these universities! If everyone can get a degree, it becomes meaningless." Indeed, there's a new tendency, isn't there, among very posh people, like Diana, and this sort of thing, to not get degrees, because everyone's got them, so they must not have one, you know? It's the reverse of the thing. Now some social critics would say they're not getting anything they need. So, there is a degree to which that which everyone has doesn't mean anything. Why are telephone boxes in mass estates vandalized all the time? Actually, they're an important resource for people. Because no one owns them, no one's bothered about them, no one cares for them, and they're the first thing to be trashed. The fact is, when wealth is socially based in that way, no one will look after it.

But I think Cowling is important, particularly for young people now who are interested in Right-wing ideas and interested in theoretical ideas. There's quite a bit about him on the Internet, reasonably respectable. And this idea that culture, civility, and high intelligence go together with Right-wing attitudes, that's very important.

The last thing I'll say is that he always believed in having a good time. He always believed in baiting the Left. He always believed in being a monster a bit, you know. People would say to him, "Don't you feel we should apologize for slavery?" And these sorts of things, and he would say, "Why? Why should we apologize?" "I could do with a few slaves here at this college," he would say. He'd say, "You want to be one of them?" And they'd sort of freeze. This is the sort of person he was. He was like the uncle at a family party that no one wants you to be introduced to. "Oh God, it's him!" That was the sort of attitude that the world had towards him, and I think that's a good thing.

And I've known a few people in my life like him, but they're very few and they're people of great power. When they enter a room, everyone else knows they're there. When they say something, everybody else listens, even if they don't like it at all. And when they've left the room, people say, "Did you hear what that chap said?" But they don't forget the person, you see. He's a sort of sacred monster, if you like.

Three people are out there like him in politics. One was Enoch Powell. One was Maurice Cowling. One was not very well known, a man called Bill Hopkins. He's Welsh, and he's one of the Angry Young Men. He's very interesting. [unintelligible] What I'll say is the importance of these great, sacred monsters of the British intellectual Right, you won't hear these names on Radio Four; you won't hear these names in *The Guardian;* you won't hear these names in *The New Statesman.* It's as if these individuals have been airbrushed out of history. But they're still there, and they do represent either a flame that can be lit for the future, or they're the echoes of the last embers of what this society once was.

Cowling wrote for *The Daily Mail.* The problem with populist discourse, though, is you have to deny that you're a monster, and you have to simplify things to such a level. But he would have written for *The Sun,* as Powell did, as Alan Clark did. Write for *The Sun,* write for *The Times Literary Supplement.* Why not? Do you know that if you write for *The Daily Mirror,* there's a red book—a red book of course for the *Mirror.* Every sentence has to be comprehensible to a 14-year-old child. No sentence must be multi-clausal, the journalists are instructed; it's on their screens. I was once taken round *The Sun* in Wapping by Garry Bushell, who was well-known for certain attitudes and certain thought. And Garry said, "I'm gonna muck in for eighty-eight grand a year, see, for writing utter . . ." In front of all the news desk.

The Sun was quite interesting, because half of them had little Dickie bow ties on. They were all public school boys. And half of them were working class white boys. And you had this odd combination. And in the background you had, you know, put their hats on or something. And they had these famous front pages, all around the office. In front of these dark areas at the back, obviously, where no one has any privacy, and everyone eating their sandwiches and watching, and this sort of thing.

Bushell took me around to look at these things, and it was quite interesting, because Powell used to write for *The Sun;* Alan Clark used to write for *The Sun.* And *The Sun* has blue book, not a red book like the *Mirror*, where every sentence must be comprehensible to a 9-year-old. A 9-year-old. And if you put script through to the staff that's got semicolons on it, they send it back and say, "What are you doing? Semicolons! For fuck's sake!" I must say, Maurice Cowling would have found that sort of atmosphere a bit difficult. But still, ideas communicate at different levels. He believes life's a hierarchy, you see. The brain's up here, and most people live down here. They're purely physical. So, what happens up here filters down to there.

I'm very pleased to address a group of young, educated people, and the future is your generation. This society will either go with a bang or a whimper in the middle of this century, within twenty to forty years. I will be 90 by then, and you'll be a bit younger than that. A major tide is coming. If we were in 1909, not 2009, a mere century ago, no one could have predicted what was coming. The First [World] War was coming, the Depression was coming, the Second [World] War was coming. There was a collapse of traditional European society in this country [unintelligible] that was coming. The social, cultural, sexual, psychological revolutions of the 1960s was coming. It's all coming. And yet no one in 1909 would really know that. And I think here in 2009, changes, totally different changes, but changes as radical are coming. Make sure your ideas influence them.

Thank you very much!

INDEX

ABOUT THE AUTHOR

JONATHAN BOWDEN, April 12, 1962–March 29, 2012, was a British novelist, playwright, essayist, painter, actor, and orator, and a leading thinker and spokesman of the British New Right. He was the author of some forty books—novels, short stories, plays for stage and screen, philosophical dialogues and essays, and literary and cultural criticism—including *Pulp Fascism: Right-Wing Themes in Comics, Graphic Novels, and Popular Literature*, ed. Greg Johnson (San Francisco: Counter-Currents, 2013) and *Western Civilization Bites Back*, ed. Greg Johnson (San Francisco: Counter-Currents, 2014).

www.ingramcontent.com/pod-product-compliance
Lightning Source LLC
Chambersburg PA
CBHW031430270326
41930CB00007B/639